WORLD
COMMUNICATION

DISEMPOWERMENT &
SELF-EMPOWERMENT

Cees Hamelink

£4-

Ⓩ

ZED BOOKS
LONDON AND NEW JERSEY

SOUTHBOUND
PENANG

THIRD WORLD NETWORK
PENANG

MS

World Communication: Disempowerment & Self-empowerment
is published by:

Zed Books Ltd.
7 Cynthia Street, London N9JF, UK and
165 First Avenue, Atlantic Highlands, New Jersey 07716, USA.

Southbound Sdn. Bhd.
9 College Square, 10250 Penang, Malaysia

Third World Network
228 Macalister Road, 10400 Penang, Malaysia
Fax: 60-4-226 4505

Printed by Jutaprint
Penang, Malaysia

Typeset by
TYPOGRAPHICS
in 10.5/16 pt.
Palatino

Zed Books Ltd.
ISBN 1 85649 393 8 Cased
ISBN 1 85649 394 6 Limp

A catalogue of this book is available from the British Library.
US CIP is available from the Library of Congress.

Contents

Preface

The idea for this book came up during a visit in July 1991 to Penang, Malaysia. The purpose of the visit was an evaluation of the activities of the Third World Network (TWN). The visit turned out to be an inspiring encounter with some very special people. Among them were Martin Khor Kok Peng, director of TWN, Mr. S. M. Mohamed Idris, coordinator of TWN and Mr. Chin Saik Yoon, my co-evaluator. I was particularly impressed with the unique combination of strong intellectual insights and concrete political action that TWN offers. The network has been very effective in establishing a local-global link between grass roots movements and international diplomacy.

Among the conclusions the evaluation reached was that the cultural issue had been so far insufficiently addressed by TWN. Yet culture is an essential tool for the integration of Third World societies in a world consumer market that primarily benefits the world's largest Trans National Corporations. Therefore, the evaluators recommended that TWN would take up research, information provision, and action in the field of cultural production.

This recommendation generated a series of discussions on possible activities TWN could embark upon. These discussions were guided by the following observations. There is an unprecedented control over global cultural and information production by a handful of transnational megaconglomerates. There is rapid proliferation of a consumerist cultural environment that serves purposes and strategies which are beyond civil democratic control. There is a need of concerted action on behalf of the world's people to democratize policy making in the field of culture and information.

Following these discussions plans were made for the creation of an international people's movement that would articulate concerns about the quality of the world's information and cultural environment. An initial exploration of possible support for these plans yielded a good number of positive comments. Among them the idea came up of holding a world tribunal that would subject today's provision of information and culture to critical inquiry. It became quickly clear that both the organization of a movement and a tribunal would require some basic document as point of reference. For this purpose a small group began drafting the People's Communication Charter. At the end of this book you will find a provisional version of the Charter. It is by no means finished and you are invited to contribute to its completion. Once we have a more complete version of the Charter the leading question remains how social movements can be mobilized to actively participate in the arena of world communication.

Important in this process of mobilization is information about the state of affairs in world communication. Issues that need clarification are questions such as which are the major trends and what do they imply for ordinary men and women?

The present book aims to clarify some of the key issues in world communication.

The production of the book was a stimulating experience, largely due to the friends in the Third World Network and in particular thanks to publisher Chin Saik Yoon.

Cees J. Hamelink
Amsterdam, February 1, 1994.

CHAPTER ONE

A Global Village?

How Global is Global?

Contemporary discourse on the state of the world frequently refers to a metaphor which is attractive, lucid, simple, and wrong. It is the projection of the world as a village.[1] When on September 29, 1992 Bangladeshi Prime Minister Khaleda Zia inaugurated the access of CNN to the Bangladesh Television (BTV) she observed that fast technological development brought about a revolution in information, turning the entire world into one village. It is indeed very tempting to use the village metaphor in situations where a network such as CNN makes TV audiences around the world eye-witness to marine landings in Somalia or the parliamentary revolt of 1993 in Moscow. This is indeed very impressive but does it warrant the use of world TV reporting as evidence that we live in a "global village"? The village metaphor suggests that world news on TV has a global scope and hereby ignores the very limited and fragmented nature of international reporting. It also suggests —in a rather misleading way that watching TV news leads to genuine knowledge and understanding about world events. Particularly striking about the village imagery is that its authors know very little about village life. In the village most people know what is going on and know each other. The opposite is true in the real world: there is more going on than ever before, yet most of us know very little about it and the majority of the world's citizens have little knowledge or understanding of each other. Even in relatively small regions such as Western Europe, there are myriad cultural differences that often obstruct meaningful communication. Although we can travel around the world and stay everywhere in very similar hotels, drink our favourite brand and watch our preferred TV show, intercultural misunderstandings remain. Gestures, words, colours, or objects have different meanings in different cultures. Also the seasoned globetrotter never ceases to be amazed about how offensive his or her own social conduct may be elsewhere in the world. The term "global village" proposes that our world is shrinking, is becoming a smaller place. This is yet another misguided representation. In a real sense, our world is expanding. There is more world than ever before in history: more people, more nations, more conflicts. It is certainly true that advances in communication and transport technology have made more contacts among people and nations a reality. Yet it is also true that around the world most people stay home. Most people lead their lives within the boundaries of the "local village". They may have a "window" on the world outside through the mass media or telecommunications. This window offers a partial view only and in any case for most people even this is not available since they live in rural poverty without electricity supply, movie theatres or transmitters. Even when they are literate, there are no newspapers or books.

The prefix "global" that pervades so many current debates, suggests a condition in which its related noun (an institution, an activity, an attitude) affects most if not all human beings and stretches out to all parts of the globe. This begs the question "how global is global"?

Taking a close look at contemporary realities, it would seem that the pretence of "globalism" is not necessarily in step with the world as it is. Today's world is certainly still a long way from conducting financial business in a global currency or governing through a global government.

What is generously termed the global economy would rather seem the economies of few OECD member states and newly industrializing countries. What is often referred to as "global communication" is virtually the transnational proliferation of mass-marketed advertising and electronic entertainment produced by a few mega-companies. As with so many other 'global' events: if there is a global information revolution, the majority of the world's population has not received an invitation. There are still very stark inequities between North and South in the access to communication hardware and software. Disparity is a clear feature of the today's global communication.

In the area of communication hardware, the world's majority of information processors and carriers are installed in a few countries only. The technology that is basic to their manufacture and up-grading is designed, developed, and controlled by the leading traders in the USA, Japan, and Western Europe. There can be little doubt that communication hardware is differentially distributed across the world.

For the North/South disparity in communication software we can look at the volume and the direction of information flows and the possibilities for generating, distributing or accessing relevant information. Information flows across the globe are imbalanced, since most of the world's information moves among the countries in the North, less between the North and the South, and very little flows amongst the countries of the South. Less than 10% of all telephone, telex and telefax traffic takes place between countries in the South.

This does not mean that there would be no demonstrations of global reverberations in which all parts of the globe are vulnerable to acts performed by some. The ecological risks provide the classical example. The environment seems to be the unique area where there is a genuine search for global solutions under way and where a level of global consciousness would seem to be emerging. Without in any way minimizing the importance of this process, it should be unequivocally stated that it is still a far cry from a genuine global understanding which would imply an acceptance and mutual recognition of socio-cultural differences and a perception of the needs of the global community as more important than those of the local community.

In reality the world's citizens have hardly begun to address the problems of the global coexistence of races and cultures. There are noteworthy upsurges in ethnic politics, communalism and nationalism. Nationalist minorities in many countries have become very active and militant.

For most of these nationalist actors local autonomy and state sovereignty take precedence over global integration. There is obviously also the rise of religious fundamentalism as a very divisive force. Interestingly enough, fundamentalism partly derives its strength from the resistance against movements towards global integration.

Global consciousness in the sense of an awareness that local events have global consequences, an understanding of the political roots of global problems, a sensitivity to the need of global solidarity, and an acceptance and mutual recognition of social and cultural differences, is largely obstructed by the ways in which the prevailing educational systems and the mass media operate.

Our educational systems pose formidable obstacles because of the highly specialised, fragmented, piece-meal approaches to knowledge. Our current university systems go a long way in discouraging any unconventional, multidisciplinary exploration. Multidisciplinarity which would be prerequisite to any attempt at global understanding and knowledge, remains a proposal in numerous academic memoranda. In reality, most universities do not train students to speak the language of sciences other than those they study. In addition, it needs to be observed that in many countries attempts at multi-ethnic and multi-cultural education have met with relatively little success.

The mass media are equally ill-equipped to enhance global consciousness. They commonly stress the priority of the local over the global, deal with problems in isolation and as incidents, leave whole parts of the globe outside their audience's reach and report in superficial, often biased if not racist ways about foreign peoples and their cultures, often exclusively highlighting their exotic features.

The International Institute of Communications conducted on November 19th, 1991 a worldwide survey on the global news agenda of that day. What emerged from the data is that the world has not come closer. In most of the news the local issues dominate. As one commentator observed, "It seems that there are many worlds on this one earth and that mostly they stay next door, minding their own business". (Chapman. 1992: 33).

The Intermediaries

Precisely, the fact that we have more world than we can personally know, makes us in unprecedented ways dependent upon a caste of professional intermediaries. They form the real priesthood of our times: telling us what is and what is not, filtering for us the truth from the lies, and providing us with an authoritative exegesis of current events.

As they stand between what we know about the other and vice versa, the quality of their mediation becomes essential to the quality of our lives. Let us briefly look at how accurate they operate. The following is obviously a limited account only and it should be recognized that there are cases in which the mass media have performed much better. However, it is important to highlight the flaws since these are not accidental but a result of common features in human perception and specific structural conditions that affect the performance of the mass media.[2]

In 1983 there was a clear prospect of a very serious famine in Africa. However, people were not yet dying like flies. Among the comments by TV station NBC on footage that showed a food distribution in Eritrea was "It is not yet a Biafra". As long as the famine did not have sufficient news or entertainment value, it could be ignored and go under-reported.

Once, however, people began to die on camera, the famine became a media-event. Then it was over-reported and hordes of anonymous Africans, without dignity, became media objects. Then also the sensationalizing began and the international media stated that some 125 million Africans were threatened by starvation. The situation was bad enough, but never over some 10 million people were actually near to starvation. In the international news media Africa was un-reported, under-reported, or over-reported.

In October 1988 three grey whales got stuck under the ice in Alaska. 150 reporters, and 26 camera crews came to report the event to over 1 billion viewers in the world. Most reports said nothing about the socio-economic conditions of the Eskimos in the same location.

In 1989 the events at Tien An Men Square took place. The *New York Times* reported 2.600 students killed in a massacre. On 21 June 1989 *The Times* admitted that about 400 may have lost their lives and that the original figure was based on rumours. There were certainly students killed in Bejing, but on Tien An Men Square never a massacre took place. Killings took place at various places in the town and according to various estimates between 200 and 1000 people may have been killed on June 4, 1989. Most of them were civilians, some soldiers, and probably some 30 to 40 students. Most media used as most important source the highly partisan Student Broadcast Station and ignored basic journalistic rules about checks and balances. (Galtung & Vincent, 1992: 240-244).

In December 1989 Eastern-European agencies reported the sensational discovery of a 4.000 people mass grave in Timisoara, Rumania. The images were shocking and looked very real. In reality, as it turned out in Timisoara never more than 150 people were killed and the grave was an old poor people's graveyard hastily dug up.

The 1991 Gulf War reporting provided prime examples of distorted mediation. Many TV stations, for example, have broadcast the videotapes manufactured for propaganda purposes in the 10 million dollar campaign conducted for the Bush administration by the Washington-based Public Relations firm Hill and Knowlton. Many important stories about the war were not reported. Videotape footage that did show that civilian damage was much heavier that the US administration cared to admit, was spiked by most TV networks. Most media selected not to report about the Allied Desert Storm casualties. Satellite photos taken on September 11, 1990 demonstrated no evidence of the massive Iraqi army threat to Saudi Arabia that President Bush referred to the same day when he tried to promote public support for the war. The news media were censored and allowed themselves to be censored.

These examples could easily be multiplied and complemented by analyses of highly wanting coverage provided by the international newsmedia of such events as the invasions of Grenada and Panama, the bombing of Tripoli, the trial of Panama's President Noriega, or the Indonesian killings on East Timor. It should also be noted that the inadequate coverage of world events is not only the shortcoming of international agencies, since very often this is compounded by the selections local gatekeepers make.

The Market-Place

The dubious quality of information provision by the professional intermediaries, is related to the structural conditions that shape the international market in which mass communication has become a large-scale commercial activity. Essential dimensions of these structural conditions are the processes of consolidation and commercialization.

Consolidation

In the past five years there has been a strong growth of various alliances between information providers from different countries. Close linkages have been built up between the most important firms in Western Europe, Japan and North America. Several of these links turned out to be preludes to mergers. In all the segments of the information market there are observable trends towards a high rate of concentration and all indications are that this will continue throughout the 1990s. The current wave of mergers in the communication industry is different from earlier processes of concentration. Today's oligopolisation is caused by very large and profitable companies that merge into mega-companies, whereas before (for example in the 1960s) concentration usually meant that big companies acquired small, loss-making firms.

In the early 1990s consolidation has definitely become the main feature of many economic sectors (such as banking, insurance, airlines) and also in the communication sector have mega-mergers become a common phenomenon. The emerging mega-industries combine programme production (ranging from digital libraries to TV entertainment), the manufacturing and operating of distribution systems (ranging from satellites to digital switches), and building the equipment for reception and processing of information (ranging from HDTV-sets to telephones). Companies are actively trying to get control over at least two of these three components. Illustrative is the Japanese company Sony that was already active in the equipment / appliance component when it acquired through Columbia Pictures and CBS-Records access to the programming component.

Commercialization

Since the early 1980s a process has begun that increasingly erodes the public sphere in many societies through the penetration of corporate interests into terrains formerly protected by public interest, such as government information, public libraries, or the arts.

Commercial sponsoring of more and more socio-cultural activities has become very popular and leads to the emergence of 'billboard' societies in which every location, institution, activity, event and person becomes a potential carrier of commercial messages. Even the United Nations have recently indicated to be interested in having some of its work supported by corporate funding. The erosion of the public sphere by implication undermines diversity of information provision.

Diversity becomes the choice markets can offer; but markets tend to offer multitude and more of the same, not fundamentally distinct goods; everything that does not pass the market threshold because there is not a sufficiently large percentage of consumers, disappears. Diversity is also under threat because the larger commercial interests of mega information providers may override the interests of independent reporting. In this context Bagdikian raises the question whether GE-owned NBC would "produce a documentary on criminality and carelessness in defence contracts, with General Electric as an obvious recent example? If it were disclosed that the company paid no income taxes during the three years of multibillion profits, and General Electric owned NBC at the time, would the network produce a documentary on inequities in the national tax system? One has to speculate, but the answer is probably a no". (Bagdikian. 1992: 210).

The Right to Remain Ignorant

The dominant mode of information provision in today's world order inflicts harm and injustice upon its ultimate clients by misinforming them, by distorting their realities, by refusing to listen to them, by keeping keep them ignorant, and by denying liability.

A serious problem, however, is that a large majority of the world's citizens show remarkably little concern for their informational environment. During the Gulf War people were kept ignorant, but many also preferred to remain ignorant. The war demonstrated that official censorship, journalistic self-censorship, and the refusal to be informed are essential components in the late 20th century information environment. As Ronald Dworkin has observed "Truth may be the first casualty of war, but some people's desire to be told the truth is a close second"(Dworkin. 1991: 2). This could be confirmed by the finding that nearly eight out of ten Americans supported the Pentagon restrictions on the press and six said that the military should exert more control. Eight out of ten said the press did an excellent job and over 60% thought the press coverage was accurate.[3]

The problem is complex: deficiencies on the supply-side and deficiencies on the demand-side mutually strengthen each other. The professional mechanisms of information mediation stand in the way of a comprehensive, and unbiased provision of information. Equally, the disinterest of the world's citizens to be fully informed, obstructs the information flows. In their preference for third-rate video and TV products and popular magazines and newspapers, millions of people state they have the right to be ignorant. As a result our expanding and complex world has a double problem: the means of information provision are highly inadequate and the users are largely uncritical.

Common Information Future

In reflecting on our common future we are increasingly concerned about the quality of our primary environment. This is the physical environment in which human life takes place. Throughout human history there is a continuous search for optimal ways of coping with this primary environment. This search leads to efforts to control nature, to mindless environmental destruction, and to careful ecological balancing. In the effort to cope with the primary environment we create the secondary environment. This environment encompasses such human efforts as the provision of information and the production of culture.

Fortunately, people around the world have become increasingly concerned about the sustainability of our primary environment and they are engaging worldwide in civil action for its defence. Yet, the ability to cope with the problems of the primary environment is directly related to the quality of the secondary environment. The more limited, one-sided, deceptive this is the less chances people have to take sensible action. Also in the sense of our informational and cultural ecology there is a serious question about a sustainable development towards the future. The report of the World Commission on Environment and Development (the Brundtland Commission), *Our Common Future*, states that sustainability requires a wider sharing of responsibilities for the impact of public decisions and increased participation in decisions that affect the environment. Only thus can we hope to develop in ways that will avoid the destruction of our common heritage for future generations. Sustainable development means we have something left for future generations.

If we condone the rapidly proceeding consolidation and commercialization of all our information provision and cultural production, there will be preciously little left for the future. Therefore, it is necessary that people mobilize themselves (for example through citizens associations, or consumer movements) to expose the deceptions and distractions of the mediators and to organize people's participation in policy making on the information environment. So far the arena of world communication has been largely ignored by people's movements.

World Communication and Disempowerment

Today's institutions and processes of world communication have a disempowering effect. This operates through censorship, deceit, victimization and information glut. The withholding and distorting of information obstructs people's independent formation of opinion and undermines people's capacity to control decisions that affect their daily lives. The very common forms of stereotypical treatment of women or ethnic minorities puts these social groups in submissive social roles. The resulting dependence, intimidation, and vulnerability victimizes and disempowers them. Disempowerment can also be caused by overpowering people with an "information glut". Just like censorship of information can be used to control people, this can also be achieved by inundating people with "a glut of unrefined, undigested information flowing in from every medium around us" (Roszak. 1986: 162). Flooding people, for example, with endless volumes of statistical information is an effective way of making people powerless.

Human Rights and Disempowerment

The present study proposes to judge disempowerment in the light of international human rights standards. The use of such external criteria is essential since often in situations of inequality both the more powerful and the more dependent actors will conveniently justify their positions by reference to some internal standard relative to their specific historical or social or cultural condition.

The normative framework defined by the respect and defence of basic human rights (as embodied in the standards of international human rights law), identifies disempowerment as a violation of fundamental human entitlements to dignity, equality, and liberty. Through the recognition of these entitlements those targeted for disempowerment can understand the illegality of wrongs committed against them. Human rights provide them with the possibility of redress and remedy. Human rights are at the starting point of all resistance against disempowerment because they give all people their unique dignity as "beings for themselves".

Empowerment and Self-Empowerment

Human rights imply both entitlements and responsibilities. This means that empowerment cannot be passively enjoyed, but has to be actively achieved and guarded. As Mahatma Gandhi wrote in 1947 to the Director General of UNESCO, "I learnt from my illiterate but wise mother that all rights to be deserved and preserved came from duty well done. Thus the very right to live accrues to us only when we do the duty of citizenship". Under international law the individual has duties towards the community. International human rights instruments articulate a duty to contribute to the protection and improvement of the human environment. They also demand a responsibility for the well-being of all people which includes both material welfare but also intellectual, spiritual and moral progress. There is also a duty to exercise political rights and a duty to promote culture.

If people want fundamental rights to be recognized and enforced, they cannot escape from the responsibility to actively contribute to the defence of these rights. People cannot expect others (the state or the media) always to defend their rights and liberties. The less alert people react to the violation of human rights, the more their own dignity comes under threat. If people do not actively engage in the battle for their empowerment, they should not be surprised to find themselves one day totally disempowered.

Notes

1. See, for example, Marshall McLuhan and Quentin Fore. (1986), *War and Peace in the Global Village*. New York: Simon and Schuster.

2. Biased representations of reality by journalists are not merely due to the specific shortcomings of this professional group. All human perception tends towards distortion. Human beings are inclined to a rapid closure of perception. This means that we often interpret complex situations with a convenient scheme by which

people are divided into manageable dichotomies (for example good ones versus bad ones) and social groups are labelled in stereotypical ways. These stereotypes are then applied to all individual members of such social groups.

3. Reported in the *International Herald Tribune*, February 1, 1991.

References

Bagdikian, B.H. (1992). *The Media Monopoly*. Boston: Beacon Press.

Chapman, G. (1992). TV: The World Next Door? In *Intermedia. Vol.* 20. No. 1.

Dworkin, R. (1991). *Index on Censorship*. Nos 4 & 5.

Galtung, J. & Vincent, R.C. (1992). *Global Glasnost*. Cresskill: Hampton Press.

Roszak, T. (1986). *The Cult of Information*. New York: Pantheon Books.

World Commission on Environment and Development. (1987). *Our Common Future*. London.

CHAPTER TWO
On The History of World Communication

Since the dawn of history human beings have communicated across long distances. Most of these communications took place within the borders of vast empires and were intended to serve their control, coordination, and expansion. Based upon relays of men and horses along imperial highways, messages could reach the most distant corners of the Egyptian, Persian, Greek, Chinese, and Roman territories. The imperial courier systems—predecessors of today's mail services—operated through word of mouth or writing. These oral or written messages were carried by runners or horse-men. An example of such an ancient telecommunication system is the network developed by the Persian emperor Cyrus (6th century BC) who had a specially appointed post-master who controlled a stable with horses and a system of couriers. When the post-master received a letter from one of the courier posts in the empire, he would arrange for a fresh horse and a courier to deliver. Exceptionally one also finds a reference to the use of fire signals for long distance communications. The news about Troje, for example, travelled in one night with fire signals over a distance of some 500 kilometres, as Aischylos reports in his book Agamemnon. There are also records of the use of carrier pigeons by the Egyptians.

The early postal systems were established exclusively for governments and they provided essential support to the empire. The Egyptian postal service that was established under Amenophis III in the 13th century B.C. provided a service that extended between the capital and all the cities of the empire.

For a long time the written transmission was impaired by its medium, the clay tablet. This changed when papyrus became the new medium to facilitate the transport of messages.

Alexander the Great appears to have used written messages and an elaborate system of messengers to keep in touch with the events in his empire. Given the primitive state of the roads and the hazards of sea traffic, communications in his vast empire must have been wanting and were probably a contributory factor to its demise.

Extensive long-distance communications are also reported from the Chinese empire during the Han dynasty (206BC/219 AD). The imperial court had established a postal system through which news on events in the empire was collected and transmitted along specified routes in the form of handwritten newsletters.

The Roman empire developed long-distance message traffic with the written medium. Over a period of almost three centuries there appears to have been regular communications across the empire of the *acta senatus* and the *acta diurna*.[1] The messages travelled across sea routes and the 49,000 miles road network the Roman empire had constructed.

Although most of these early long distance communications have probably been fairly limited to regional traffic, there have also been early exchanges across the world through trade, diplomacy, and religion.

Illustrative cases are the encounters between the Chinese and the Indian civilizations. "Historically, there were few military or diplomatic relations between them; rather, their communications with one another were filtered through middlemen and intermediate cultures; their encounter was pacific —the movement of ideas, words, books, things—rather than invasion, infiltration or conquest; the flow was mainly one way, from India to China" (Wright. 1979: 205). In this cross-cultural encounter Buddhism was brought from India to China through the travels of the Chinese monk Fa Hsien (399-414 AD).

Much in advance of the formal diplomacy that originated with the European society of states (after the 1648 Peace of Westphalia), there have been international diplomatic exchanges. The early Egyptian, Hellenic,

Greek, Chinese and Byzantine state systems had developed sophisticated forms of international diplomacy. There is evidence that Egyptian diplomacy began under the eighteenth dynasty (1580-1350 B.C). "The Pharaoh sent his representatives to neighbours in the Mediterranean by Phoenician-made oared boats or by Egyptian ships known by such names as 'Appearing in Memphis' or the 'Sun-Disk Lightens' " (Tran Van Dinh. 1987: 12). The Greeks had roving ambassadors and regularly hosted diplomatic emissaries from abroad. China under the Han dynasty and later under the Tang dynasty (618-906 AD) maintained extensive diplomatic contacts with other territories. Among them were the Syrians, Persians, Koreans, Japanese, Tibetans, and Vietnamese. As ambassadors of their faith, the early Christian apostles travelled great distances throughout Asia Minor, Greece and the Roman empire. By the year 200 AD missionaries had also gone to Egypt and Africa. In the middle of the 3rd century Christians could be found in Western Europe, the Armenian Kingdom, Arab countries, Mesopotamia, and India.

There have also been early forms of international public relations as attempts to cultivate images in the service of foreign policy. The use of propaganda messages in international relations was well known in antiquity. Alexander the Great had what amounted to a PR unit. "Reports written to serve his ends were sent to the Macedonian court, multiplied there and disseminated with propagandistic intent" (Kunczik. 1990: 73).

Early trading also provided important carriers for the exchange of information and culture. Trade and information routes connected Asia, the Mediterranean, Africa, and the Pacific. The spice and silk routes linked Mesopotamia and Iran with India and China. Gold was extracted in West Africa and transported across the Sahara to North Africa and the Middle East. Before Vasco da Gama's travels from Portugal in the fifteenth century, trading took place between what is to-day Zimbabwe and China (for Chinese pottery) and India (for gold and ivory). Before Captain Cook travelled to the South Seas, Melanesian and Polynesian seafarers had sufficient geographical information to make very long sea voyages. The early courier systems expanded throughout the Middle Ages and from the 12th century on an organized information traffic emerged in Europe.

Although it is likely that most people did not travel, there was a growing number of travellers to far destinations. They included crusaders, missionaries, artists, traders, and pilgrims.

New cultural centres emerged in Europe and they began to communicate with each other. From the 12th century some European universities, notably the University of Paris (Sorbonne) and several monasteries developed their own systems of couriers. These couriers became professionals with special rules on payments, working-time and sanctions in case of malpractice. In the 14th century the Hanseatic League developed a communication network for its commercial purposes.

Oral media of transmission remained important carriers of foreign news in the 13th century. Town criers reported for example the news about the taking of Milan or the treaty with Pope Clement VII in Paris (Stephens. 1988: 40). Towards the late Middle Ages networks of correspondents and intelligence agents had begun to operate as professional carriers of political, military, or ecclesiastical information along well organized traffic routes. Usually the towns that had become key trading centres, also were the chief news centres. Through Vienna came dispatches from the Balkans; Augsburg processed news from Italy, Switzerland, southern Germany and the East (*via* Venice); in Cologne messages from France and the Netherlands converged with news from Britain, which came by way of Antwerp. Material from Russia and surrounding countries passed through Danzig and Breslau, while Hamburg was the arrival point for news from Scandinavia and the whole of northern Europe. By 1600 the demand for such information had reached the level at which it had become economic to find printed means for distributing it. (Smith. 1979: 19).

In the 16th century the first postal system covering several European countries was initiated by Franz von Taxis. On March 1, 1500 King Philips I appointed Von Taxis *captaine et maître de nos postes*. Against an annual salary he was to maintain postal traffic between the Low Countries, Germany, France, and Spain. In 1516 Von Taxis was appointed by the emperor Maximilian I Chief Postmaster and was given the sole privilege of operating the postal system in the Low Countries.

In the 16th century authorities in Spain and Germany permitted private mail services. In England the post was established as a national system (16th century) and the postmaster primarily delivered for the King who had monopoly control. The service was not in the first place public, although messages for private clients were delivered since they brought in profits.

Gradually the European postal services began their real large scale development in the Renaissance as more and more governments set up postal services for public use. Rulers such as Frederick III of the Holy Roman Empire, Louis XI of France and Edward IV of England were committed to more efficient postal services. In this historical process the postal services and the news services became distinct entities.

It can be argued that the 15th century saw the first organized distribution of information to other nations. This was initiated by the political community wanting to spread knowledge about itself and to gather intelligence about foreign countries. Most monarchs had their private networks of foreign correspondents and international spies.

There was for instance extensive knowledge about Italy in England through a vast network of diplomats and agents. This was also the beginning of the deliberate distribution of information to other nations. In the 15th century handwritten newsletters began to spread news among the countries of Europe. The newsletter about Edward IV reclaiming his crown in 1471 was published in English and French and was distributed with long time delays. In another example, a copy of a newsletter sent by an Italian in Constantinople in 1481 at the time of the death of Sultan Mohammed II was made for Edward, Prince of Wales only in 1483.

In the 16th century Europe's trading community began to develop cosmopolitan interests and with this a strong need for information from abroad. For the Venetian merchants information about safe arrivals of ships or their losses was crucial to market prices. Prices of wheat were also determined by military news, such as the movements of the Turkish fleet.

Members of the trading community created their own information systems, and in 1536 the first trader's news agency was established in Venice. The financier Philip Eduard Fugger created the Fugger letters and between 1568 and 1604 these hand-written letters were spreading international information of general and financial interest (Stephens. 1988: 75).

In the 16th and 17th century the first European newspapers were created and they in their own way furthered cross-border communications. The Venetian gazette travelled to London in the mid-16th century and contained foreign news, for example information from Vienna about the proceedings of the Turks (Stephens. 1988: 153). Much of the international messages were about politics or the military. By 1566 weekly handwritten news sheets were produced in Venice but the scope of their distribution is unclear.

There is some evidence that through handwritten news sheets information about Italy circulated in Germany by the late 16th century. The oldest printed newspapers, for instance the *Courante uyt Italien, Duytslandt, &c.*, published at Amsterdam had foreign reports. By the mid-17th century there were some eight weekly or bi-weekly printed publications in Amsterdam that provided the cosmopolitan trading community with foreign news of special interest to them. Not only about Italy and Germany, but also about America, Africa and Asia.

It was also in the 17th century that the Reformation and the Counter-Reformation using the new technology of movable type printing began to push cross-border communications further. The messages of Reformation preachers spread across Europe and the Catholic Church began to expand its mission to other continents, such as Latin America and China. When Pope Gregory XV in 1622 founded the *Sacra Congregatio de Propaganda Fide*, the congregation received among its briefs the call to propagate the catholic faith to the New World. In 1627 Pope Urban VII established a special training centre, the *Collegium Urbanum de Propaganda Fide* where catholic propagandists received their training before spreading their religious ideas across the world.

In the 17th century a cosmopolitan academic community emerged and information about scientific discoveries began to travel across borders through newspapers, books and journals. Scientists began to organize themselves in groups, such as the Royal Society in England. The mail was the most common vehicle for cross-border communications but was of course highly inadequate to keep the expanding scientific community informed.

In the second half of the 17th century scientific periodical publications arrived, such as the *Journal des Savants* in France (1665) and the *Philosophical Transactions* in England (1665). Isaac Newton's *Principia mathematica* (1687) was reviewed in the *Journal des Savants*, in the *Bibliothèque* (published in Holland) and in the *Acta Eriditorum* (published in Leipzig).

Throughout the 18th century into the early 19th century newspapers did attempt to bring foreign news but continued to be hampered by the war conditions and weather conditions of the time which caused enormous delays and inaccuracies in reporting.

Long distance communications moved at a very slow pace. Letters from Europe to India would take routinely almost eight months and sending and receiving a reply could take as much as two years. Particularly with regard to people and events in faraway places the information would tend to be distorted and often focus on the exotic and bizarre. French news sources would into the early 19th century refer to the population of distant countries as "savages" (Stephen. 1988: 219).

The 18th century saw the performance of one of history's greatest propagandists, Napoleon. "He engaged in a veritable propaganda battle with the rest of Europe, a battle of big words. Against Britain, which was waging a caricature campaign against Napoleon, a battle was fought in the press in which Napoleon, however, reached mainly the French people and the inhabitants of areas occupied by France. Napoleon's press policy in the occupied areas showed itself, for example, in press guidelines being decreed in the German kingdom of Saxony after Napoleon's victory under which anything 'which might be objectionable to the French imperial court must be avoided with the greatest care'. . . But Napoleon also communicated selectively with foreign countries. The open appeal to the civilian population was something fundamentally new. Thus in 1796 he directed a manifesto to the Tiroleans to give up 'the hopeless cause of their emperor' ". (Kunzcik. 1990: 75).

It was only in the 19th century that the collection and distribution of international news became a large-scale operation. The British Post Office sold summaries of articles in the foreign press to the newspapers in London. In 1832 the first private international news agency was established by Charles Havas in France using carrier pigeons and the semaphore telegraph (Stephens. 1988: 259).

In 1848 the New York newspapers (Associated Press) agreed to share expenses for the collection and distribution of foreign news through a chartered steamer (that would meet ships from Europe at Halifax) and the telegraphic traffic of information from Boston (where the steamer would arrive) to New York.

By 1855 Bernard Wolff began his service in Berlin and in 1858 Paul Julius Reuter started a service for the London papers. The most crucial technological breakthrough came with the invention of the telegraph by Samuel Morse. The first transmission took place on 4 September, 1837 and on 27 May 1843: the first telegraphic connection between Washington and Baltimore was established. The first underseas cable began operation in 1866 between Valencia and Newfoundland. The first telecommunication connection using the human voice was on January 25, 1878 in New Haven. Around the turn of the century there were some two million telephone connections operational across the world. Before the end of the 19th century the possibility of wireless transmission was explored by Alexander Stepanowitsch Popow and Guglielemo Marconi who used knowledge generated by Heinrich Hertz. In 1901 Marconi could send radio signals over a distance of 3,540 kilometres between England and the United States. Around 1906 the first human voice was transmitted through radio broadcast.

In the course of the 19th century international diplomacy began to use the mass media as instruments of foreign politics. This was part of a change from the conventional form of secret diplomacy to a new type of more open diplomatic negotiation. The newspapers played an important role in this change, but it was particularly the development of wireless radio which significantly increased the potential for this new form of diplomacy. More and more diplomats shifted from traditional forms of silent diplomacy to a public diplomacy in which the constituencies of other states were directly addressed.

Public diplomacy became to some extent a form of aggressive propaganda. During the First World War an extensive use was made of the means of propaganda. This psychological warfare did continue after the war had ended. International short wave radio began immediately after the First World War. In 1926 there were in Europe already some 26 stations that could provide international transmissions. By 1923 American radio amateurs had discovered the long range features of high frequencies and conducted two-way transatlantic communications. Soon states began to use HF for international broadcasting. The Dutch began with broadcasts to the East-Indies colonies in 1929, the French started their overseas service in 1931, the BBC followed suit with an Empire Service in 1932, the Belgians in 1934. In 1930 the USSR began using short wave broadcasting to reach foreign audiences.

During the Second World War international propaganda was conducted on a very grand scale. Both by the Nazi-regime and the Allied Forces. The American Office of Strategic Services used for example popular music: German translations of American songs were recorded by artists such as Marlene Dietrich and broadcast by clandestine radio stations. The texts were adapted to propagandize the American "way of life". After the war international propaganda continued to operate as an integral dimension of international relations. The Cold War between the Super Powers became in fact a "war of words": a propaganda and disinformation war.

Since 1945 the most important factors that shaped world communication were the international political developments, the world economy, and technological innovations.

World Politics

After the Second World War the world system expanded in important ways and even the mere increase in number of actors had an impact on the growth of world communication. Between 1956 and 1989 the number of United Nations member states grew from 80 to 159, the number of intergovernmental organizations increased from 132 to 300, and the international NGOs expanded from 973 to almost 4,621.[2] However, the most dramatic impact on world communication was caused by the two major confrontations in the arena of world politics: the East/West tension and the ensuing Cold War and the North/South gap in economics, culture, and communication.

The Cold War brought a confrontation with extended disinformation, psychological warfare, propaganda, an expanding intelligence community, and the militarization of outer space.

Cold War: Disinformation

After 1945 international propaganda evolved as an integral dimension of international relations. The Cold War between the Super Powers was in fact a "war of words": a propaganda and disinformation war.

The US Central Intelligence Agency (CIA) is known to have been active in the field of disinformation for many years. Some sources have estimated that the CIA may have been spending an annual amount exceeding 1,000 million dollars for such activities. It is likely that the CIA began its international media operations in 1948 when it did try to influence elections in Italy. Between 1966 and 1975 the agency operated its own features service, the Forum World Features supplying information to over a hundred newspapers, among them the *Washington Post* (Kunzcik. 1990: 196). The CIA has used journalists for various intelligence operations, mainly reportorial in nature. This was revealed in 1977 by Carl Bernstein in an article in *Rolling Stone* and by a series in the *New York Times* by John M. Crewdson.

As the *New York Times* commented, "Since the closing days of World War II, more than 30 and perhaps as many as 100 American journalists employed by a score of American news organisations have worked as salaried intelligence operatives while performing their reportorial duties". In October 1977, the Associated Press Managing Editors Association condemned the CIA use of journalists and called upon the Agency to provide public assurance that it had stopped such practices. In December 1977, the CIA promised not to enter into clandestine relationships with journalists.

In 1980 however, CIA director Admiral Stansfield Turner disclosed that since 1977 he had personally approved of the use of journalists for secret intelligence work in three separate cases. At the convention of the American Society of Newspaper Editors in April 1980 he stated that no journalists were at the time actively employed or paid by the CIA, but if a situation presented itself in which he felt such a practice was justified, he would not hesitate recruiting journalists.

Apart from this direct use of journalists as "spooks", the Agency has over the years owned, subsidized and influenced a host of newspapers, news agencies and other media. It is not possible to determine precisely the extent of this operation, let alone to assess how successful it may have been. It can be established, however, that since the early 1950s the CIA has owned or subsidised over 50 newspapers, news services, radio stations and periodicals, both in the USA and abroad. In addition, some 12 non-US news organisations have been infiltrated by paid CIA agents and more than 10 large publishing houses have published over 250 books financed or produced by the CIA. In the 1960s, for instance, publisher Praeger brought some 16 CIA-financed books on the market. The Agency also supported such communist periodicals as *The Daily Worker*. At least 12 CIA officers worked as full-time reporters with American news media, where they planted fabricated stories or distorted true stories. Such stories were regularly picked up by the Associated Press and UPI wire services which spread them globally. An important part of what was proclaimed to be Nikita Khrushchev's secret speech to the 20th Communist Party Congress in 1956, when it was published in Western news media, was manufactured by CIA experts. The CIA prepared a version of the speech to which it added 34 paragraphs about foreign policy which were missing from the copy the agency had managed to get hold of (Kunczik. 1990: 195).

In the 1950s, the CIA planted a bogus story about Chinese troops on their way to aid the Vietnamese communists in their battle with the French. In the 1960s, the CIA provided false information on the strength of North Vietnamese forces and on the rate of their infiltration into South Vietnam. From 1970 until the brutal end of his regime in 1973, Chile's democratically elected President Salvador Allende was the victim of CIA-planted stories in even such prestigious newspapers as the *New York Times* and the *Washington Post*. In 1986 the Reagan administration carried out a disinformation campaign against Libyan head of state Ghadaffi. (Kunczik. 1990: 196).

The news media played an important role in the field of disinformation through the uncritical acceptance of information provided to them. On important occasions, the media were willing to trust sources such as the Pentagon too easily, for example in the case of comparisons between the relative military strengths of the USA and the Soviet Union. The media have often too quickly adopted military notions such as "winnable, limited nuclear war", and have copied mystifications as proposed by military strategists on the precision of military missiles.

A lack of critical analysis may have reinforced the position of those calling for increases in arms expenditures. This was quite explicit at the time of the Iran hostage crisis and the Soviet occupation of Afghanistan. Practically all US media responded to this with references to the relative weakness of USA *vis-à-vis* Soviet weapons production, the incapacity of the USA to deter the Soviet Union and the need to spend more on armament. *Time* magazine, for example, commented in October 1979: "The Pentagon wants more and it has a strong case".

In 1980 and 1981, prominent US newspapers like the *Washington Post* and the *New York Times* carried articles on the possibility of limited nuclear war, without seriously raising the question as to what exactly "winning" such a war would mean.

Cold War: Propaganda and Psychological Warfare

Since in the nuclear age international combat could hardly be fought militarily, at least between nuclear states, the arena moved from armed conflict via diplomatic negotiations towards propaganda and counter-propaganda. As a result the United States and the Soviet Union were engaged in a propaganda war.

On 28 May 1980, James Wright, Republican spokesman in the US House of Representatives, stated that "the USA cannot risk losing the battle for minds in all countries of the world". This "battle for minds" was indeed supported by the US government with impressive resources, but equally important were the contributions made by private initiatives and the mass media. The Committee on the Present Danger (established in 1976), for example, conducted propaganda against treaties on the reduction of nuclear arms and gave special emphasis to the alleged Soviet desire to conquer the world. Among the distinguished members of this Committee were Jeane Kirkpatrick, Paul Nitze, George Schultz, and William Casey. In 1978, the Committee, together with the American Conservative Union and the Coalition for Peace through Strength, spent US$200,000 to broadcast a film on "Russian power and American myth" via 200 television stations as part of a campaign against ratification of the SALT 2 agreement. In 1982 the Centre for Strategic and International Studies at the University of Georgetown, Washington, hosted a *Reader's Digest*-sponsored meeting, during which an increase in psychological warfare was recommended. Among the participants were Jeane Kirkpatrick, Henry Kissinger, and Zbigniew Brezinski.

A special contribution to the propaganda war was also provided by the US President Ronald Reagan. Illustrative was his reference to the Soviet Union as "the focus of evil in the modern world" in his speech to a meeting of evangelical Christians, March 1983, in Orlando, Florida. This speech, meant for a domestic audience, did certainly not fail to heighten Soviet insecurities about their adversary.

The Soviet Union was just as heavily engaged in propaganda. Soviet international propaganda found its origins in the Communist International

(Comintern) set up in 1919 as an aggressive disinformation agency. Among the purposes of post-war Soviet international propaganda were spreading the idea of the revolution in other countries, breaking up existing alliances against the Soviet Union by exploiting differences in interests between the allies, and weakening individual Western countries by stirring up internal tensions there (Kunczik. 1990: 214). Also the KGB has used journalists in many countries to influence public opinion and official decision making. In 1959 a special department for disinformation was established. A great variety of manufactured stories were put in foreign newspapers across the world. Among the very many illustrations is the forged speech that Jeane Kirkpatrick was alleged to have given to the United Nations in her function as the US ambassador.

The text was distributed on the eve of a non-aligned conference in Delhi, India (1983) and suggested a balkanisation of India and firm support of the US administration for South Africa (Kunczik. 1990: 219). Soviet propaganda was stepped up particularly since 1975. According to the Soviet government, this became necessary when Western countries began using extensive propaganda against the Soviet Union after the signing of the Helsinki Final Act. The Soviet authorities called their activities an "offensive in counter-propaganda". This offensive used among its weapons political cartoons in the newspapers *Pravda* and *Izvestia*, arguing that the Western press is an instrument of aggressive NATO strategists, that Western journalists are allies of the CIA, that they maintain the myth of a Soviet threat and that the political programme of US President Ronald Reagan is full of deceit, violence and bribery. One of the key official spokesmen in this counter-propaganda was the Soviet Defence Minister Marshall Dimitri Ustinov. He stated repeatedly that all activities of the United States were geared towards the establishment of superiority *vis-à-vis* the Soviet Union and that American politics were dangerous and deceptive. Moreover, he pointed out rather emphatically that the imperialist powers would have to be aware that in case they prepared for nuclear war they could not evade a crushing pre-emptive strike by very alert Soviet forces.

An important actor in international image-making was also the United States Information Agency (USIA) established in 1953. The USIA was renamed in 1978 the International Communication Agency, and in 1982 its name reverted to USIA. President Kennedy defined the USIA mandate as, "The mission of the United States Information Agency is to help achieve United States foreign policy objectives by:

1. Influencing public attitudes in other nations, and

2. Advising the President, his representatives abroad, and the various departments and agencies of the implications of foreign opinion for present and contemplated United States policies, programs, and official statements" (Kunczik. 1990: 184).

The USIA operated libraries, book programmes, production and distribution of films, and the radio station Voice of America. Part of the international information activities were also visitor programmes to the USA, seminars, academic exchange programmes, and cultural presentations. The USIA was also actively involved in the manufacturing of news about such events as the Bay of Pigs invasion in 1961 or the shooting down of the South Korean airliner KAL 007 in 1983. In 1993 the Agency had a US$1.2 billion budget and some 8,000 employees. In the light of the changed East-West relations, the Clinton administration has announced a major reorganization of the USIA to bring it in line with post-Cold War realities. The planned restructuring would affect the publication of magazines, the overseas facilities of the agency and in particular its broadcast activities.

Cold War: the Expanding Intelligence Community

Spying: In the East/West relations after 1945 the interception and registration of international information flows became an important part of military activities. The gathering of international intelligence took place, for example, in Menwith Hill (UK) where the American National Security Agency had established the largest listening post in the world. Employing a staff of 800 people, all trans-oceanic telephone and telex traffic from and into Eastern Europe were monitored here.

International spying has taken a number of different forms. NATO listening posts in Turkey, for instance, monitored all radio broadcasts by the Soviet armed forces (in Sinope), collected seismographic data on subterranean nuclear explosions (in Belbasi), or monitored the movements of Soviet satellites through radar (in Diyarbakir). Spying also took place through observations from space. Both the USA and the USSR operated a series of spy satellites through which data could be remotely sensed about such diverse objects as the movement of troops, the launching of rockets, the building of launch bases or the next grain harvest. The IMEWS and Keyhole 11 satellites employed by the USA, for example, have collected very precise imagery of Soviet territory and have observed some 400 Soviet tests of strategic and tactical missiles.

In January 1985 a new type of "eavesdropping" satellite was put into orbital position through the Space Shuttle. This military application of the Shuttle was originally supposed to remain a secret, but was leaked to the press and as TASS commented, the Shuttle programme had now assumed "an open military nature".

The SIGINT satellite was the first of a new generation of spy satellites to function in a geosynchronous orbit (some 22,000 miles above the equator) with the capacity to monitor a broad range of Soviet electronic transmissions such as the communication links between Moscow and Soviet military bases. In the late 1980s the USA launched the Teal Ruby satellite which employs millions of infrared sensors, each of which focuses all the time on one specific point through a telescopic lens. They note and report each minute change and its direction immediately. Also a new generation of Keyhole satellites (the KH 12) with IKON (improved keyhole photo reconnaissance) was developed. Responding to the various US advances in the field of satellite spying, the Soviet Union since 1984 employed its "listening" satellite the Kosmos 1603.

Warning Systems: The gathering of intelligence on the opponent became in the nuclear era more important than in any earlier period. The destructive power and the velocity of nuclear weapons did create the necessity to develop vertically integrated organizations in which nuclear forces and warning systems could be linked together. This linkage was the logical consequence of the fact that in any nuclear policy the key element is early warning. The need to get timely information about a pending nuclear attack by the opponent is absolutely essential. This implied the development of a comprehensive network of channels through which information could be collected and processed. Such a continuous supply of information was meaningful only if there was an organization that could at all times respond to the information in an alert way. Therefore, in 1953, the North American Aerospace Defence Command (NORAD) began to design such an organization. By the end of the 1970s, both the USA and the Soviet Union had fully implemented vertically integrated warning and weapons systems that could be readied for warfare in a matter of minutes. The communication systems for military intelligence and early warning that were implemented were of an impressive scope and capacity. Developments in computer technology enabled both the USA and the USSR to collect and process millions of signals. It became possible for the Soviet Union to monitor, record and identify thousands of private telephone conversations in the USA and for the United States to collect such seemingly trivial information as laundry lists of Soviet submarine crews. The development of satellite technology made a spatial resolution capacity possible that helped to identify objects of 30 centimetres diameter from an altitude of some 250 kilometres.

It is evident that this capacity to collect ever more pieces of information significantly increased the warning value of the intelligence system. The collection of a myriad of small details also increased the possibility of false interpretations of ambiguous signals and the combination of isolated signals into a threatening pattern. Such a combination could lead to a situation of higher alert which consequently would trigger a response by the opponent and this action-reaction chain could spiral into a crisis situation.

Vulnerability: A special problem was caused by the strong degree of vulnerability of intelligence gathering and warning systems. A well-known illustration is the so-called Electromagnetic Pulse (EMP) that results from a nuclear explosion and that has a destructive effect on electronic equipment. EMP was first recognized in 1962 when the USA exploded a hydrogen bomb 248 miles above the Pacific Ocean, at which precise moment the street lights went out in Hawaii, 800 miles away. The explosion of a small nuclear bomb at an altitude of some 375 kilometres would cause a disruption of electronic systems within a range of 2,000 kilometres. It can easily be imagined how this could lead to a separation of military headquarters and field forces (a sort of decapitation) which would render an international conflict practically uncontrollable.

Equally important was the possibility that the vulnerable ground stations that are central to satellite communications would be destroyed by enemy attack. Ten such stations were critical to most of Western military communications. Another example were the 25 public telephone switching centres that take care of a large part of North American military communications. These stations were the likely targets of Soviet submarines stationed close to American coasts. As a matter of fact, most missile warning systems depended on commercial telephone lines.

For the data to reach NORAD from satellite-based sensors, they had to go through a satellite receiving station in Australia, via oceanic cable (vulnerable to malfunction and destruction) to a telephone switch in Sunnyvale, California (located 18 kilometres from a major earthquake fault), and then through public telephone lines to NORAD.

Intelligence and warning systems were also "jammed". The US spy satellites (the Keyhole 11 satellites for example) found their signals occasionally jammed when they travelled over Soviet territory. A form of laser beam interference from the Soviet base at Saryshagan was the likely cause.

Cold War: the Militarization of Outer Space

From the beginning of the "space age" both the USA and the Soviet Union proposed that space should be used exclusively for "peaceful purposes". Various American presidents, among them Eisenhower, Kennedy and Johnson have stated this. The Soviet leadership, among them Khrushchev and Bulganin, also clearly expressed support for this aim.

TABLE 1. *Operational Military Satellite Systems.*

SATELLITE SYSTEM	COUNTRY	YEAR
AF SATCOM - Air Force Satellite Communications System	USA	1979
DSCS - Defence Satellite Communications System	USA	1966
FLTSATCOM -Fleet Satellite Communications System	USA	1978
NATO - Communications Satellite Project	NATO states	1967
U.K. SDCN - Skynet Defence Communications Network	UK	1969
U.S.S.R. COSMOS Military Satellite Network	Soviet Union	n.a.
U.S.S.R. Gals - Military Satellite Network	Soviet Union	n.a.

The problem in the space debate has been the definition of what constitutes "peaceful" versus "aggressive" use. Some held the opinion that all military operations are by definition non-peaceful. For them, even reconnaissance by military satellite for arms verification purposes was not permitted. Other positions claimed that all defensive operations, such as arms control through space objects, are peaceful. Otherwise, they argued, even civilian remote sensing, which could be used militarily, would have to be outlawed. Whatever the political positions and interpretations may have proposed, since the early 1960s space increasingly became the arena of military activities. Of all satellites launched in the past decades, over 75 % were intended for military purposes (see for an overview Table 1 and Table 2). Military satellites carry out critical reconnaissance, warning and commu-nications functions. Between 1958 and 1978, the US government spent over

US50,000 million on military space projects. In 1981, the annual expenditure for such projects totalled over US$7,000 million (see Table 3).

TABLE 2. *Types of Military Satellites 1981.*

TYPE	COUNTRY	NUMBER
Photosatellites for detection	USA	235
	Soviet Union	538
	China	3
Electronic satellites for exploration	USA	79
	Soviet Union	125
Satellites for early warning	USA	22
	Soviet Union	25
Satellites for ocean-monitoring	USA	18
	Soviet Union	32
Navigation satellites	USA	39
	Soviet Union	58
Communication satellites	USA	118
	Soviet Union	366
	NATO	5
	UK	4
	France	2

Source: Bh. Jasani (ed), *Outer Space—A new dimension of the arms race*, London, 1982.

Most space projects were "passive" systems meant for replacement of more conventional observation and communication systems. In warning systems, the sensors on board the satellites would observe the enemy's attack and send the information to computer systems that are linked to the launching bases of intercontinental missiles. Launching of enemy missiles is observed by detecting the heat radiated during the firing of the rockets. These satellites formed crucial targets in case a nuclear power would consider a first strike. In order to attack the passive satellite, active systems were developed, the so-called "killer satellites" or anti-satellite weapons (ASAT) that would incapacitate the enemy's satellites. Development and testing of ASATs began in 1967 by the USSR. During the 1970s, the Soviet Union tested its anti-satellite satellites against targets in space. In the late 1970s and early 1980s, the USA embarked on its ASAT programme in order to overcome the Soviet lead.

TABLE 3. *Expenditures for Military Space Projects, U.S.A., 1981.*

PROJECT	EXPENDITURE (US$ MILLION)
Navigation satellites	190.7
Communication satellites	817.5
Warning satellites	273.6
Geodetic satellites	9.9
Meteorological satellites	90.3
Development space vehicles	726.1
Earth stations	286.2
Research space programme	564.0
Administration space programme	1.952.4
Espionage satellites	2.500.0
TOTAL:	US$7.4 billion dollars

Source: *The Defence Monitor* (1982). Centre for Defence Information.

At the 1983 session of the Conference on Disarmament, the Soviet representative stated that the USSR would not be the first to use an ASAT and his delegation proposed a unilateral moratorium on ASAT launches as long as other states would also refrain. In January 1984, the USA launched a new type of ASAT into space, prompting *Pravda* to comment, "Now that a massive programme to develop anti-rocket space weapons has been undertaken on the President's own instructions, the chance of reaching agreement are lessened even more" On 19 May 1985, President Chernenko of the USSR called for a ban on all space weapons and accused the USA of rendering space "into an arena of aggression and war".

The militarization of space received generous support from US President Ronald Reagan, particularly through his speech of 23 March 1983. In this speech the proposal was launched for a space-based ballistic missile defence system that would make present nuclear weapons "impotent and obsolete". As the President dramatically stated, "What if free people could live secure in the knowledge that their security did not rest upon the threat of instant US retaliation to deter a Soviet attack, that we could intercept and destroy strategic ballistic missiles before they reached our own soil or that of our allies ?" This "hope for the future" would turn the nuclear doctrine of mutually assured destruction (MAD) into mutually assured security.

Meanwhile a major research effort had begun, somewhat comparable to previous large-scale projects, such as the development of the A-bomb (the Manhattan project) or the moon landing (the Apollo project). For an initial 5 years, a budget of some US$25,000 million was presented to carry out research into fields such as high energy lasers, charged particle beams, tracking and guidance systems, high velocity launchers, and computer systems. To achieve the stated objectives, this defence system would have to be capable of intercepting some 2,000 Soviet land-based intercontinental ballistic missiles in the so-called "boost phase". During this phase which lasts some 5 minutes the engines of the rockets are firing. Following this, the launched missiles may each release some 10 separate warheads, thus multiplying the targets to some 20,000. The additional complication in this phase would be the problem of distinguishing the real from the decoy warheads. This second phase lasts some 20 minutes. Then, when the missiles re-enter the atmosphere, there is another minute before they explode. Even if they explode at high altitudes, or even if only a few missiles reach their targets, the damage would be beyond imagination. The Strategic Defence Initiative (or SDI, as this "Star War" scenario was officially called), was strongly promoted and supported by the Reagan administration.

The North/South Confrontation

After the SecondWorld War yet another international tension began to develop between the developed industrial countries in the North and the largely rural developing countries in the South. Most of the latter, so-called Third World countries, had been former colonial territories of the centre countries of the North. Between 1945 and the late 1960s a large number of new, post-colonial states emerged in Asia and Africa. In their struggle to become sovereign entities, they confronted in addition to political and economic dependencies, the cultural legacy of former colonial relations. The first generation of post-colonial nationalist leaders was intent on creating national integration in state structures that were internally threatened by the existence of multiple nationalities (often artificially thrown together) and externally beleaguered by a forceful cultural diplomacy enacted through Western foreign policy and business interests.

In the early 1950s the first collective performance by the post-colonial states began. In those years the political cooperation between African and Asian countries, in particular, was at stake, as the 1955 Bandung conference demonstrated. In the 1960s this coalition was extended to include the Latin American countries, which brought economic problems to the agenda.

Actually, since the mid-1960s, the non-aligned movement has given increasing attention to strategies for the development of economic links among the countries of the South. Alongside the non-aligned movement, the so-called Group of 77 came into existence at the First UNCTAD confer-ence in 1964. Both groups found themselves caught in the ambivalent position of the South: between strengthening horizontal linkages and coping with the remaining links with the former colonial powers. That these latter links had an important cultural component became clear in the early 1970s. In particular, the non-aligned summit in Algiers (1973) began to extend South- South cooperation to the area of cultural development.

An important component of the background history leading to the information debate, was also the expectation (particularly during the First United Nations Development Decade) that the technological achievements of the developed countries would contribute decisively to the resolution of the global disparities between the rich and the poor. It was assumed in the 1960s that technology, which had lifted the advanced industrial nations to unprecedented levels of material wealth, could do the same for the poorer nations. The transfer of the latest and the best from the developed countries to the developing countries, did seem the most adequate instrument for development. Towards the 1970s the tone of the development debate became notably less optimistic. Technology had been transferred, albeit mainly in the shape of end-products and often with disadvantageous conditions for the recipients, but sharp disparities in access to and distribution of technology remained and the basic problems of structural poverty and exploitation had not been resolved.

In the field of communication technology the results of processes of transfer did suggest, by the late 1960s, that the primary beneficiaries (of telephone, educational television, and satellite communications) had been foreign manufacturers, foreign bankers and national administrative and military elites. In most countries the introduction of modern communication technology had not resolved any of the basic problems, but had rather added to the obstacles for a process of independent and self-reliant development.

In most developing countries the pattern was that advanced technology was not primarily introduced to meet the basic needs of the people, but as the support system for the expansion of transnational business. The needs of this business system added yet another vital component to the environment in which the information debate originated. Since the early 1950s there had been a rapid rise of transnational industrial and financial companies. These spread their affiliates across the globe and began marketing, advertising and trading in many of the developing countries. As part of the growing world business system, the branch of information/communication conglomerates developed into one of the leading sectors. Increasingly, the world's flows of news and entertainment began to be controlled by ever fewer companies, often closely interlocked among themselves and with other industrial and financial interests.

Throughout the 1970s the world political debate on information issues (which took place primarily in UNESCO) developed in the context of an economic dialogue between the North and the South which was largely inspired by the threat of a North/South confrontation over oil prices. In 1974, the United Nations General Assembly adopted the Declaration and Programme of Action on the Establishment of a New International Economic Order. In the same year the Charter of Economic Rights and Duties of States was adopted. In 1976 the UNCTAD IV at Nairobi accepted the Integrated Programme for Commodities and a new financial institution was created to support the effort to stabilize the world's commodity markets, the Common Fund.

In terms of political practice all this meant very little. As a matter of fact, by the end of the 1970s the North withdrew from this dialogue as the oil-threat had subsided. The UNCTAD V in 1979 at Manila did mark the point at which the North-South round of negotiations on a fundamental restructuring of the world economy effectively ended. A few efforts to renew the dialogue in the early 1980s (such as the Cancun Summit, 1981, or the UNCTAD VI in 1983) met with no success.

To this "real world environment", should be added a specific dimension of the history of the United Nations which goes back to the late 1940s. The origins of a persistent controversy about the solution of global information inequality are to be found in the immediate post-War years at the time of the incipient United Nations. This controversy is rooted in an early "division of labour" within the United Nations system that embodied a distinction between political and technical tasks in dealing with international information questions. Already early in the history of the United Nations system it was a rather common claim among the Western member states that the specialised agencies of the UN should be technical rather than political. Political issues were to be dealt with by the UN General Assembly, whereas the other agencies, and among them UNESCO were supposed to provide technical assistance to the implementation of the normative principles elaborated by the political body.

In the field of information this meant that the UN General Assembly would be responsible for news and freedom of information, and UNESCO would deal with the improvement of the technical conditions for news production and exchange and promote the free circulation of educational and cultural materials. As a result of this division of labour, UNESCO began to implement a programme of technical assistance. In 1957 a UNESCO report on the global "information famine" motivated the United Nations General Assembly to request the Economic and Social Council (ECOSOC) in 1958 to formulate a programme for the development of communication and information media in the developing countries. ECOSOC invited the specialized UN agencies to contribute to this programme and in 1962 ECOSOC recommended to the General Assembly that the UNESCO programme would be integrated within the efforts of the First United Nations Development Decade. The technical assistance programme thus established and implemented lasted throughout 1960s and made UNESCO into a forum of consensus on information matters.

In the 1970s, however, the non-aligned countries recognized that this technical assistance did not alter their dependency status, that "information famine" persisted and that in fact their cultural sovereignty was increasingly threatened. They therefore opened the debate on the need of normative standard-setting regarding the mass media. The key agenda issue for this debate was the demand for a new international information order. The information gap between the North and the South which was very much at the centre of the debates on this non-aligned demand, did remain throughout the 1980s an essential feature of world communication. Information disparity is till the present day characteristic for the current North/South interaction.

In the area of communication hardware, the world's majority of information processors and carriers are installed in a few countries only. The technology that is basic to their manufacture and up-grading is designed, developed, and controlled by the leading traders in the US, Japan, and Western Europe. Communication hardware is differentially distributed across the world. Several examples can illustrate this.

Together all the developing countries own only 4% of the world's computers. 75% of the world's 700 million telephone sets can be found in the nine richest countries. The poor countries possess less than 10%, and in most rural areas there is less than one telephone for every 1,000 people. There are more telephones in Japan alone (with a 121 million population in 1988) than in the fifty nations of Africa (with a 1988 population four times the size).

In 1988 some 30 poor countries have no newspapers at all, while in 30 others there is only one. By contrast, Japan has 125 daily newspapers and the USA has 1,687. The average for European countries is 39 newspapers and the African average is less than 3 newspapers per country. In the USA the dailies have a circulation of 268 copies per 1,000 inhabitants and in Japan this is 562 per 1000. The European average is 288 and the African average is 16.5.

The rich countries which represent some 30% of the world's population, account for almost 80% of the world's press circulation, and the poor countries with some 70% of the world's population have only 20% of total newspaper circulation. The developing countries have only 5% of world imports of newspaper and periodicals and only 3% of world exports.

Europe produces an average of 12,000 new book titles every year. African countries less than 350. Europe has an average 1,400 public libraries per country where the public has free access to information. African countries have an average of 18 libraries per country.

The world average for radio set ownership is 330 per 1,000 population. In the rich countries this is 911 per 1,000 and in the poor countries 142 per 1,000. For example, the density of radio sets in the USA is 2,100 per 1,000 and the average for African countries is 134.

In 34 periphery countries there are no TV sets at all. The world average for TV set ownership is 137 per 1,000, the gap is 447 per 1,000 for the rich countries and 36 for the poor.[3]

For communication software we can look at the volume and the direction of information flows and the possibilities for generating, distributing or accessing relevant information. Information flows across the globe are imbalanced, since most of the world's information moves among the countries in the North, less between the North and the South, and very little flows amongst the countries of the South. Less than 10% of all telephone, telex and telefax traffic takes place between countries in the South. Flows between the North and the South tend to be one-way. Estimates suggest that the flow of news from the North to the South is one hundred times more than the flow in the opposite direction. In the mid-1980s, Europe broadcasted 855 hours yearly to Africa, while Africa broadcasted only 70 hours back to Europe. Imbalances are evident in television imports also, so that West European countries import an average 33% of their programmes while African countries import 55% of their total TV programmes .

If we look at different kinds of information, we find other hidden kinds of imbalances. In the main, the flow between North and South consists of "raw", unprocessed information coming from the South while the North provides ready-made information packages, and as with manufactured goods the considerable value added by processing translates into higher costs for the South if it wants to buy it back in processed form.

In the field of scientific and technical information only 3% of the world's research and development takes place in the South. Only 1% of the world's patent grants are held by nationals of the poor countries, since in most of those countries the technology patents are held by a small number of transnational corporations.

Most of the world's scientific and technical information is produced and owned by individuals and companies in the North. The South Commission observed in its report that characteristic of developments in the past decade is, ". . . the increasing monopolization of technological progress by transnational corporations in the North" (South Commission. 1990: 218). As the sweeping pace of innovation revolutionizes societies, "the principle of science as the shared heritage of mankind is being systematically eroded. Knowledge is becoming increasingly privatized, and the South is being excluded" (South Commission. 1990: 218, 219).

Full access to financial and trading information is the privileged property of a few private enterprises in the North. It needs only little imagination to establish that the poor countries are seriously handicapped in accessing information about the complex and swiftly changing dimensions of the international finance system. For example they do not receive timely and reliable information on rates of exchange or rates of interest. They have no access to the international financial information brokerage circuit and the vast and expensive systems for the processing and distributing of this information.

Financial information flows across the globe as computer data through the communication networks of large banks and as economic news through news agencies and newspapers. Financial data are controlled by large international banks that own and/or operate international computer/communication systems. These banks also enjoy privileged access to vital financial information through more traditional means. This means that in trade negotiations, for example, the South is at a considerable disadvantage when bargaining, often having fewer skilled negotiators and less useful information.

Resource information is another area where the North has enormous advantages, mainly through data collection about global natural resources by remote resource sensing techniques that use sensors on board of satellites in the polar orbit. This technology has developed since the early 1970s and offers today a vast amount of very useful images. Remote sensing is currently applied to crop monitoring, forestry, hydrology, oceanography and mineral exploitation. The user-community of remotely sensed data is growing, but hardly in the South. The technological advantage of access to the means to collect and process such data can be illustrated by the usefulness of early information about mineral deposits or crop diseases. Through satellite technology coffee traders in New York know more about imminent Brazilian coffee harvests than do the Brazilian coffee producers. Similarly large international fishing companies know more about the whereabouts of tuna shoals off the West Coast of Africa than do the local fishermen, and they use this information to land the best catches.

There are also severe international imbalances in a more public form of information, news. Four leading world agencies largely control the international flow of printed news AP, UPI (bankrupt in 1992 and acquired by the Middle East Broadcasting Co.), AFP and Reuters. While for visual information the dominant sources are Reuter TV (formerly Visnews) and WTN, and to lesser extent BBC World Service and CNN.

The average daily news production of the world agencies is AP 17 million words per day, UPI, 14 million, Reuters 1.5 million and AFP 1 million. By way of comparison, the only world agency with a special interest in developments in the poor countries, Inter Press Service, produces daily an average of 100,000 words. World news is almost exclusively about events in the North. If the South is reported at all, this is usually because there is a link with the superpower conflict (Afghanistan or Nicaragua), a threat to core interests (the Iran-Iraq war and the Iraqi invasion in Kuwait), a sensational drama (floods in Bangladesh , murders in Sri Lanka, famine in Ethiopia), a historical relation (news about ex-colonies), or some exotic dimension (aboriginals in Australia, prostitutes in Thailand).

Elaborate South-South information routes existed long before the late 15th century, when European colonial expansion began. This had its origins in pre-history and spread with the growth of Egypt, China, India and Mesopotamia. Information routes linked Asia, Africa, the Pacific and the Mediterranean shores. By the second half of the 18th century a fully fledged international colonial economy had materialized, which re-routed information from South-South to South-North. Most information flows began to follow the axis of colonial power.

The resulting paucity of South-South information traffic is a serious obstacle for horizontal forms of co-operation among developing countries. Most international routes still reflect colonial times and link the countries of the South only via the North. Several international conferences have recognized this. The United Nations conference on Technical Co-operation among Developing Countries (TCDC) in 1978 at Buenos Aires, declared as one TCDC objective, the increasing and improving of "communications among developing countries, leading to a greater awareness of available knowledge and experience as well as the creation of new knowledge in tackling problems of development". Similarly, the high level Conference on Economic Co-operation among Developing Countries at Caracas (May 1981) emphasized the crucial role of information exchange and communication capacity, particularly for the promotion of trade among developing countries.

The differential access to the management of information has put the developing countries at a serious disadvantage in the world political-economy. Their lack of capability to collect, process and apply information to their specific requirements compromises their national sovereignty. Increasingly the capacity to influence the deployment of their resources was shifted to foreign entities in extra-territorial locations. Today's world communication discrepancies are critical factors in hampering the self-reliant development of the South. The contribution of the South to world communication has not improved over the past decades. Some developing countries have grown as export markets for communication hardware, but this has been mainly due to foreign investment by transnational corporations. In so far as developing countries have increased their import capacity for communication technology, they have become more dependent upon the economic forces of the North.

Transnationalization

In the early 1950s Western industrial production began to move towards the countries of the South in search of cheap labour and new markets. With the combination of rising labour costs and the development of such technologies as containerization and satellite communication, this transnationalization of industry became both a necessity and a possibility.

The proliferation of industrial investment required the coordination of widely dispersed units of transnational corporations. In order to coordinate the dispersed affiliates and markets of large transnational corporations modern telecommunications became an indispensable instrument.

On average a large corporation with sales of US$1billion would spend some US$14 million annually on telecommunication bills alone. This was corroborated with the worldwide establishment of production centres and markets: the "global shopping centre" emerged and with it the worldwide proliferation of advertising and marketing. Moreover, during the 1970s many of the major transnational corporations began to organize their own information provision to support their worldwide marketing, advertising, and public relations needs. The largest transnational corporations (the Fortune 500) established an in-house capacity for the production of film, TV and videopresentations that could easily compete with major international audiovisual networks. Responding to the merging wave of critical questions directed at the legitimacy of modern corporate business the latest technical innovations for international "image-cultivation" were employed. Between 1975 and 1984 US corporations increased their budgets for corporate advertising from US\$ 305 million to over US\$1 billion (Pavik. 1987: 49). By 1985 over three-quarters of major US corporations used the services of international PR firms mainly for marketing purposes (Wilcox. 1989: 397).

The international expansion of industrial production since the early 1950s did equally bring an export of related services such as travel, finance, marketing and advertising. Also the transnationalization of banking drastically increased the need for international information networks.

An essential feature of the post Second World War world economic development was the emergence of an expanding services sector. This sector grew in the national economies of most Western industrial countries and also came to account for a significant portion of world trade. This implicitly caused a growth of cross-border information traffic, as so many activities in the services sector are in fact trading of information or are supported by information technology. Such illustrations as international travel, tourism, banking, credit card use or tourism make this abundantly clear. The economic development in the affluent part of the world also resulted in the increase of private consumer expenditures. The arrival of the consumer society did indeed contribute to a significant expansion of information handling across borders with the proliferation of demands for education, entertainment, and tourism. With the expansion of the services sector, information handling grew since many activities in the sector are information intensive. By 1980, the total world trade in services amounted to some US$400 billion, which represented over 20% of overall world trade.

Related to the overall economic expansion was the development and proliferation of a transnational communication industry across the world. This industry adopted several striking features such as strong alliances within the industry and between the industry and such sectors as the defence establishments of major industrial countries. The industry also became identified by its need for large volumes of finance capital, the role of media tycoons, and the development of consolidated mega-conglomerates.

Interlocking Interests

Throughout the 1970s the communication industry became largely controlled by a network of some 80 very large transnational corporations with strong interlocking interests. On the surface it looked as if the international production and distribution of communication goods and services was carried out by a small, but competitive groups of contending parties with diverse interests. Closer analysis, however, revealed that the information industry was characterized by an intricate web of interlocks. This had various dimensions. Between the major communication corporations there were direct interlocks in the form of joint ventures, joint ownership of subsidiaries (such as between Philips and Siemens with Polygram, between NCR, Control Data, and ICL with CPI, between Honeywell and Control Data with MPI), stockholdings (such as in the case of General Electric holding 11% of the stock in Toshiba, Philips holding 24.5% of the Grundig stock, Saint Gobain-Pont-a Mousson holding 10% in CII Honeywell-Bull and 331/3 % in Olivetti), licensing, supply, sales, or production agreements (such as between Fujitsu and Siemens, Honeywell and Nippon Electric, Xerox and Mitsubishi, Olivetti and Hitachi, AEG/Telefunken and Thomson/Brandt), joint directorates (such as between IBM and Time, Honeywell and GE, Interpublic and CBS, McGraw Hill and Sperry Rand, ICL and Plessey).

In addition to these direct interlocks there were important indirect interlocks, mainly through directorates. Such interlocks implied that directors of
corporation A would meet directors of corporation B across the boardroom
tables of X other corporations.

TABLE 4. *The 25 US Communication Corporations With the Largest
Defence Contracts for Military Equipment, 1982.*

CORPORATION	DEFENCE CONTRACT (U$ MILLION)	% OF REVENUES
Mc Donnell Douglas	5,617	77
General Electric	3,562	13
Lockheed	3,498	53
Boeing Co.	3,239	36
Hughes Aircraft	3,140	N.A.
Rockwell	2,690	36
Westinghouse	1,492	15.2
Litton Industries	1,316	26
Honeywell Inc.	1,217	22
I.B.M.	1,196	3.2
Sperry Corp.	1,148	20
R.C.A.	995	12
T.R.W.	867	17
Texas Instruments	839	19
A.T.& T.	753	1.2
G.T.& E.	567	4.7
Singer	549	21
L.T.V.	548	10
I.T.& T.	442	3
North American Philips	409	11
Motorola Inc.	288	7.6
Burroughs	214	5.2
Control Data Corp.	175	4
Hewlett Packard	153	3.6
Transamerica	138	3.2

Source: US Department of Defence/*Fortune.*

This meant that what seemed to be major competitors in the information industry such as IBM and AT&T had 22 indirect routes through which they could "supply convenient conduits for possible private solution of the public debate between monopoly and competition in the telecommunications industry", according to the report of a US Senate Subcommittee (Hamelink. 1983: 24). The indirect interlocks provided, as the report commented, "substantial opportunity for direct policy discussions and potential understandings among these major competitors" (Hamelink. 1983: 24). Such discussion and understanding reduced genuine competition to what was termed "courteous competition." No genuine free market developed and very little space was made for newcomers.

TABLE 5. *Communication Corporations With Large Defence Contracts for Research and Development in the USA, 1982.*

CORPORATION	DEFENCE CONTRACT (US$ MILLION)
Rockwell	1,962
Boeing	1,112
Mc Donnell Douglas	796
Hughes Aircraft	668
T.R.W.	482
General Electric	481
Lockheed	370
Westinghouse	275
Honeywell	237
I.B.M.	228
Sperry Corp.	155
G.T.&E.	138
R.C.A.	136
I.T.&T.	125
Texas Instruments	93
Litton	71
Singer	71
Motorola Inc.	43
TOTAL:	7,443

A particular development was the combination of interests in hardware and software sectors. The industry counted a number of corporations that were active in both areas. Illustrations were: the US firms—RCA, Xerox, IT&T, Litton, Singer, Lockheed; the UK firms–EMI, Rank, Decca; the German firm, Siemens, and the Dutch firm, Philips.

There were also direct and indirect interlocks between leading firms in hard ware sectors and similarly firms in software sectors. Significant were: IBM, interlocks with Time, CBS, ABC, New York Times, McGraw Hill, Washington Post, Interpublic, and MCA; General Electric, interlocks with Time, CBS, ABC, New York Times, and McGraw Hill; RCA, interlocks with CBS, ABC, Time, Interpublic, and Disney Productions; EMI, interlocks with Thomson, Pearson, Reed, and ATV/ACC; Philips, interlocks with MCA, Polygram; Siemens interlocks with Polygram, and Bertelsmann.

In terms of the essential external interlocks of the industry, those with the military deserve some detail. The military leadership had a more than passing interest in the type of information technology which was to be developed. In most of the recent communication innovations, military inputs have played an important role. One can observe this in the development of the electronic computer, the integrated circuit, radar, lasers, computer software (the language COBOL), the integration of optical and electronic systems (for the development of an extremely rapid operating computer using light instead of electrons), and the so-called "superchip". Regarding the latter: in 1984 the US Defence Department paid US\$170.2 million to IBM, TRC and Honeywell for the development (by 1989) of a chip of 0.5 micron size for deployment in weapons systems. In some cases the military took the initiative and proposed to industry the development of a specific technique. In other cases, research already under way was subsidized through considerable funding in order to reduce the time span between commercial availability and military application. This has led to a mutual dependency between the military leadership and large contractors for military projects. Among the latter are several of the leading international communication companies. In fiscal 1982, the US Ministry of Defence spent a total of US$125,000 million on civilian contracts for military products. Some US$14,000 million were allocated for electronics and communication systems. An amount of approximately US$14,000 million was spent in 1982 on research and development. Out of this expenditure, US$2,800 million were utilized for electronics and communication systems. The largest defence contractors from the US communication industry are listed in Table 4 and Table 5. Among the 100 largest US defence contractors (providing over two thirds of all military equipment) are a number of communication companies which in 1982 won over 50% of the defence contracts. Among the 100 transnational communication industries that control most of the world's information production and distribution, at least 30 have close links with military interests. They are among the largest contractors for both equipment and research (see Table 6). These military purchaser-industrial supplier interlocks had a number of consequences. Among them were:

1. The choice of techniques to be developed became largely defined by military interests. The research and development (R&D) effort needed for technological innovation is highly capital-intensive and makes the industrial manufacturers of technical products largely dependent upon external funding. The military have been very generous in providing such funds, evidently with an indication of the type of equipment they need. During the First World War the US military needed transmitters, receivers and detectors. The electronics industry provided them and consequently boomed as a result of large defence contracts.

2. The funding of R&D through selected industrial corporations strengthened the degree of industrial concentration. The availability of funds to a limited number of large firms created an important advantage for these companies over other contenders in the market. As a result, markets were increasingly dominated by ever fewer firms.

3. The invention of useful civilian "spin-offs" from military R&D (for example ceramic ovenware resulting from space research) usually fulfilled

TABLE 6. *Top Corporations in the International Communication Industry With Strong Direct Military Connections.*

CORPORATION	COUNTRY
Mc Donnell Douglas	USA
General Electric	USA
Lockheed	USA
Rockwell	USA
Litton	USA
Honeywell	USA
I.B M.	U.S.A.
Sperry Corp.	USA
R.C.A.	USA
T.R.W.	USA
A.T.& T.	USA
G.T.& E.	USA
Singer	USA
L.T.V.	USA
I.T & T.	USA
Burroughs	USA
Transamerica	USA
Control Data Corp.	USA
Philips	Netherlands
Siemens	Germany
AEG/Telefunken	Germany
Ericsson	Sweden
E.M.I.	UK
Plessey	UK
I.C.L.	UK
Decca	UK
Cll-Honeywell Bull	France
Thomson-CSF	France
Hachette/Matra	France
Texas Instruments	USA

the function of partial legitimation of excessive defence spending. The fact
that all such spin-offs could have been developed at far less expense without
military research was more often than not conveniently ignored.

Capital Intensity

In the telecommunication industry, labour intensity has largely been ex-
changed for capital intensity. This sector used to employ large numbers of
factory workers, maintenance crews, and systems operators. Increasingly
new technologies made them redundant. Electronic exchanges in the telephone system, for example, could be manufactured, maintained, and
operated by a few people with specialized computer technique skills.
Between 1974 and 1977 large telecommunications equipment manufacturers, such as Philips, Siemens, and Western Electric reduced their work-force
by 5 - 25%.

A crucial factor in the increasing capital needs in this sector were the costs
of R&D, similar to those in the data processing sector and the electronic
components industry. High expenditures were made for the exploration
and implementation of such techniques as optical fibres, lasers, and micro-
processors.

In 1977, the combined average percentage of sales spent on R&D for U.S.
aerospace, data processing, and electronics was 4.1%, as compared to 2.5%
in another R&D intensive industry, the chemical industry. In 1979 R&D
expenditures in the US data processing sector were considerably greater
than in all manufacturing. In the Federal Republic of Germany, the electri-
cal/electronics industry spent 6.4% of sales on R&D in 1978, which com-
pares with 4.7% in chemicals, 5.7% in automotive, and 3% in engineering
and mining. Some of the leading FRG firms spent more, like Siemens with
10% and AEG/Telefunken with 7% of total turnovers.

On a global scale, it can be estimated that R&D expenditure for information technology amounts to some 30% of the world research and development budget. This demands large funds and attracts large investments, both

from private and governmental sources. Among large investors there is increasing interest in corporations' R&D figures.

In the communication industry the more traditional mass media sectors are also capital intensive and in need of increasing investments for their fixed costs. Large fixed capital is needed in the publishing industry, e.g. . . . , for the costs of paper and printing ink. Over the last decade, prices for the paper used for most magazines have doubled and printing inks have, over the past five years, increased by some 40 % . Some cannot cope with this demand and are forced out of the business. Illustrative of this market expulsion is the case of United Press International which faced mounting losses (up to some US$7 million) and its owner E.W. Scripps Co. was forced to seek a buyer. After a series of tumultuous years UPI was finally declared bankrupt and auctioned. In 1992 the agency was bought by the Middle East Broadcasting Co.

Product promotion is a major expenditure in the sector for recorded music, where promotion budgets for top selling categories such as rock music have increased three times over the past five years. Another aspect of capital intensity in the record industry is the rapidly increasing front investment which, for example, in a rock music LP album has risen from US$100,000 to US$250,000 during the 1980s. This is caused by the costs of sophisticated recording equipment and the high royalties for musicians and fees for producers. MCA, for example, paid Elton John US$8 million for a five year contract in the mid-Seventies. Warner Brothers guaranteed Paul Simon US$13 million in 1978 for his transfer from CBS. CBS is reported as having signed an US$8 million contract with Paul McCartney in 1979 for three albums. Today top performers like Prince or Madonna ask and get astronomical fees for their recordings.

Capital investment for production is also on the increase in the film sector. With the increasing volume of fixed capital, the risks for capital to be invested in film production became greater. This, in turn, caused greater control by financiers and less likelihood for small, independent producers to get credit. In the 1980s the costs of the average feature film production began to exceed the US$15 million mark. The increasing costs of production are due to the considerable expansion of fixed capital in the industry, i.e., capital to be invested in the means of production, such as studios, technical equipment, special effects. There are also rising costs for marketing, employment of "stars", and distribution. The latter is possible only through very expensive international networks, and also exhibition has become more capital intensive with the emergence of luxurious cinemas. Production costs in Hollywood continue soaring. In 1990 the average feature film costs over US$30 million. Star performers also became increasingly expensive: Stallone for example received US$20 million for Rocky V .

The communication industry developed as a growth sector, a capital intensive industry and as a very profitable enterprise. This profitability of the industry did attract new investors: large companies that formerly had little or no operations in the information field. Examples include Boeing, McDonnell Douglas, Fiat, Coca Cola, Exxon, and Matra. As the information producers became integrated into large industrial conglomerates, their industrial policies were predominantly guided by economic concerns.

Ownership Structures: Institutional Investors and Tycoons

In the communication industry, like in other industrial sectors, the institutional investors are key players. They include pension funds, insurance companies and banks. In the past decades institutional investors have become increasingly active in the management of companies through their stock ownership and through their participation on boards of directors. In many of the largest communication companies over half of the stock is controlled by these institutional investors. Among them the international banks are most prominently present. It is obvious that institutional investors are primarily interested in a maximum return for the interests they represent.

A characteristic element of the communication industry is the considerable number of cases in which one individual or one family group , often identical or strongly related to the original founder, has much of the voting stock. Significant owner control exists in those corporations in which one individual or one family group holds over 10% of the voting stock, and no other stockholder owns a similar proportion. This type of control occurs in almost a quarter of the hundred largest communication corporations. Well-known examples of "tycoons", or "media-moguls" are the late Robert Maxwell, Rupert Murdoch, Robert Hersant, Leo Kirch, Sylvio Berlusconi, or Sumner Redstone. Characteristic for this type of control is the direct involvement of individual owners in the daily operations of their media. There are, however, many indications that point to serious financial difficulties presently confronting these "tycoons". In order to operate on today's world market in a competitive way implies the need of enormous investments and considerable financial risks. As a matter of fact many of the large companies are heavily in debt (see table 7) and they may only escape bankruptcy if they merge with other companies. In sheer economic terms the survival chances of information companies that become part of larger industrial conglomerates are better. It needs to be pointed out, however, that the expected 'synergy' does not always materialize. The Japanese companies Sony and Matsuhita, for example, which added vast software interests to their hardware manufacturing have so far not seen remarkable increases in their sales of consumer electronics as a result of their acquisitions. The media-giant Time-Warner is still struggling with an enormous debt and with considerable clashes among its various units such as the hostile antagonists Home Box Office and Warner Brothers.

Concentration

Characteristic of the communication industry has been a high level of concentration in all its sectors. In most sectors this was already the case in their early history. Between the two world wars international advertising was already largely in the hands of two agencies: J. Walter Thompson and McCann. The film industry has had a strong degree of concentration since the 1920's, when eight major companies practically controlled production, distribution, and exhibition (Paramount, Warner Bros., 20th Century Fox, Loew's Inc., United Artists, Universal Pictures, RKO, and Columbia). From the outset the development of the film industry has been determined by a tendency towards decisive influence upon the market for maintaining and expanding profits. "This oligopolistic structure not only controlled the US industry, it also already dominated the world industry and drew a signifi- cant proportion of its revenues and profits from the non-US market" (Hamelink, 1984: 34)

TABLE 7. *Debt Burden of Mega-Companies.*

COMPANY	DEBT (US$ BILLION)
Time-Warner	16
News Corp. (Murdoch)	8
Maxwell Communications	3
MTV	2.4
Hachette	1.7
Bertelsmann	0.7
Paramount	0.5

Sources: *Television Business International*, March 1991 and *Business Week*, October 4, 1993.

For the record industry Chapple and Garofalo give the following ac- count: "The industry did not begin with a number of small companies gradually becoming to be monopolized by a few powerful firms. From the beginning a few, two or three, large firms have accounted for a majority of industry volume. The major reason for this is that the two biggest record companies have since 1900 been linked to phonograph firms and since the thirties to large broadcasting and electronics corporations" (Chapple and Garofalo. 1977: 92).

The international production and distribution of news has been domi- nated by four large agencies since late in the 19th century. The beginning of concentration in the data processing sector is of more recent date. In the early 1950's the US industry supplied more than 95% of the world market. Among these US firms one company had the uncontested leader position: IBM. During the sixties its market share was estimated to vary between 66 and 72%.

The market control by a few companies was reinforced by the wave of mergers in the 1970s, then further strengthened by the development of conglomerates throughout the 1980s, and then consolidated in the global markets of the 1990s. During the 1980s many companies in the communication industry became either part of larger industrial conglomerates, or became communication conglomerates themselves. Examples of such communication conglomerates are companies like: Bertelsmann (with books, records, TV, video, and printing), Rupert Murdoch's News Corporation Ltd. (with newspapers, magazines, TV, and film) and Time/Warner Inc. (with magazines, books, records, cable TV, and film).

Examples of industrial conglomerates with considerable investments in communication are companies like General Electric (manufacturing washing machines, light bulbs, ceramics, components for weapons systems, computers, telecommunications, and running TV network NBC), and Silvio Belusconi's Finivest (real estate, insurance, department stores, TV networks, advertising, and newspapers).

Economic Significance of the Industry

By 1976, the total revenues for the 86 leading transnational communication corporations amounted to US$147 billion. The major part of this came from the sales of hardware goods—48% from telecommunication equipment, 20% from data processing, and 13% from consumer electronics. In 1980 the total world market for communication hardware and software could be estimated at some US$350 billion or some 18% of total world trade.

In 1986 the total world market for equipment (consumer electronics, telecommunication equipment, computers, semiconductors), services (telecommunication services, data processing services, and advertising), and mass media (broadcasting, publishing, film and recorded music) did constitute a business of over US$1.600 billion.

The telecommunication services market was valued in 1991 at approximately US$150 billion and was expected to grow to over US$600 billion dollars by 2000.[4] The telecommunication equipment market was estimated at US$102 billion dollars.[5] The world market for advertising was in 1991 worth some US$224 billion. The world sales for recorded music grew from 12 billion dollars in 1981 to 24 billion dollars in 1990. Within three decades the information industry became big business for big companies and big markets. In 1992 it was predicted that by 2000 the international media industry could reach the US$3 trillion mark.[6]

Technological Innovations

A series of technological innovations has influenced the development of world communication since 1945. Among them were new reprographic techniques, video technologies (television, videotex and homevideo systems), audiotechniques and integrated circuit technology. Most essential to the expansion of the scope, volume and speed of cross-border information traffic have been the technologies of electronic information processing and telecommunication.

Computer Technology

Early antecedents of today's computer technology can be found in the Chinese calculator, the "abacus", that has been used since 2600 B.C. More recently were the adding machines developed by Pascal (1647) and the wheel to perform the four arithmetic operations designed by Leibniz (1673). The fundamental logical principles of electronic computing were proposed by George Boole in 1854 and in the same century Charles Babbage dreamt of the first mechanical computer. Babbage designed his "Analytical Engine": a computer that could be programmed for various purposes. The machine was never constructed but its visionary design contained the four components essential to the later electronic computer : the storage of data, the manipulation of data, the transportation of data from storage to manipulation, and the mechanism for inputting and outputting data.

The first electromechanical calculator was developed by Howard Aiken in Harvard University with the support of IBM. This was in 1939 and the computer was called MARK I. The first electronic computer: the ENIAC was designed by J. Presper Eckert and J. W. Mauchly of Pennsylvania University with the support of the U.S. Ministry of Defence. This computer—developed during the Second World War—started the "first" generation of electronic computing that was characterized by the enormous size of the systems and their reliance on large numbers of vacuum tubes. In this first period the mathematician John von Neumann drew the blueprint upon which most computer architecture is still based. In his design the computer consists of a central processing unit (where the arithmetic and logical operations are performed) and a storage unit (the memory where the data and the instructions for operations are kept). The storage unit is an electronic medium that contains data in a binary code (as chains of 0's and 1's). The computer transports data at high speed back and forth between memory and central processing unit. During the 1950s the "second" generation emerged due to the application of an important invention: the transistor. This device replaced the vacuum tubes and its small size, reliability, speed of operation, and reduced energy consumption, marked enormous progress. Now computers could be developed with more sophisticated and versatile programming capacity.

The early 1970s witnessed the advent of the "third" generation computer. Developments in micro-electronics created the capacity to implant large numbers of transistors on very small surfaces. Thus thousands of electronic circuits could be integrated on a few square millimetres of silicon: the so-called "chip". It became possible to put the complete central processing unit of a computer on one "chip": the microprocessor. The first microprocessor was manufactured by the firm INTEL in 1971 and in 1975 the first computer based on the microprocessor (the "microcomputer") was marketed. The sophisticated, flexible, and relatively inexpensive "personal computer" of the 1980s is often identified as the "fourth" generation. Characteristic for this period of technological development was the further miniaturization of electronic components, the exploration of new conduct-ing materials, the testing of new techniques for faster electronic switching, and the expansion of memory capacity. Probably most decisive, however, were the attempts to improve computer software: the languages in which computers can be instructed to perform certain operations. The develop-ment of computer software was particularly focused on the challenge to overcome the limitations of the Von Neumann architecture. This basic computer design allows a linear, sequential processing of information, but excludes parallel, associative processing. The latter is needed in order to render computers more "user-friendly", i.e. more accessible in common daily language. A radical departure from the Von Neumann computer would introduce the "fifth" generation. The current race in computer technology to develop associative, "intelligent", and easy-to-use electronic systems is headed by Japan and the U.S.A. with Western Europe following suit.

Over the past decades computers have significantly increased their performance capacity. From simple electronic calculators they have devel-oped into multi-purpose systems with a large number of applications. They have also improved their speed of operation and their reliability. At the same time they have become easier to handle, smaller in size and lower in price. This has caused a wide proliferation of computers in the world primarily in the industrialized countries, but recently the developing countries have also become growing import markets for computers. The value of installed computers in the world has increased from US$12.7 billion in 1960 to US$424 billion in 1978 and expanded to US$990 billion by 1988. Between 1980 and 1988 the numbers of computers in the world increased from 9,000 to almost 2 million. The fastest proliferation took place in the field of the personal computer. Average growth rates for the USA and Western Europe are estimated between 30% and 40% annually. Also the interest for the utiliza-tion of computer services is growing at average rates of 15% annually. Although the significance of computer technology is already evident, the full market potential for computing remains to be developed. It would seem that a further expansion of computer use would demand the development of really user-friendly computers. Despite the application of new programming languages that certainly improved machine-user interactions, computers are still a far cry from accessible consumer electronics, such as radio and television. Moreover, the majority of the world population (in the developing countries) has presently access to only some 4% of the world's computers.

Telecommunication Technology

Initially, computer technology and telecommunication technology were explored and applied in distinct ways. For almost eighty years telecommunication technology generated and upgraded technologies for transmissions between people-centred "transducers", such as telephones, facsimile machines and television systems. In its development it added to transmission and transducers the technique of switching which made networking possible. When electronic data processing became available it was applied to telecommunication for the enhancement of its efficiency, particularly in switching systems.

In the course of the 1950s the two technologies became integrated. Computer-communication networks were created consisting of computers with communication lines attached to them which could link computers to other computers or to terminals . Centralized networks were designed in which data could be transported for processing, storing or forwarding to centrally located computers . Also distributed networks were constructed with data traffic between decentralized computers or terminals. Transmissions through such networks commenced with the first circuits for defence systems and airline reservations. During the 1960s and 1970s networks were also increasingly applied for international banking, credit control, data banks and intergovernmental cooperation.

It seems a fair expectation that with the growth of volumes of business information, the utilization of computer-communication networks will face still further expansion in the years ahead. The convergence of telecommunication and computer technologies into "telematics" implies that the communication and processing operations that used to be performed by separate systems can now be executed by one integrated system. This system facilitates a significant increase in volume, rapidity, reliability and complexity of information handling.

The capacity of this system will be further enlarged with the growing sophistication of computers and telecommunication carriers. In this respect particularly important are developments in integrated circuit technology , computer programming, satellite technology and optical fibre technology.

The widening capacity of computer-communication networks has been made possible by a number of technological developments which have considerably increased the performance capacity, the accessibility and the compatibility of computing and telecommunication facilities.

The traditional telephone networks have greatly enhanced their capacity for data traffic through such techniques as modems and multiplexors. Modems modulate digital computer signals into analogue telephone signals and demodulate analogue signals into digital signals. In their development they have assumed complex control tasks that go way beyond mere modulation and demodulation. Multiplexors are devices that facilitate the transmission of two or more messages simultaneously over a single transmission line. For the expansion of networks they are essential as they permit the clustering of information flows for transmission through common record carriers. The development of optical fibres has further increased the data transmission capacity of the telephone network. They make it possible to transport digital signals through light over glass-fibre cables. An eight millimetre optical fibre cable has about the same capacity as a twenty centimetre copper cable (some 30,000 telephone calls) and is more resistant to conditions that cause disturbances in traffic through the copper cable.

A vital technological development has also been packet-switching. This technique brought the telecommunications facility to a level of comparable efficiency with the data processing facility. In 1975 the Advanced Research Projects Agency of the US Department of Defence initiated the transmission of data among disparate, remote computers and terminals through a network of over 50 packet-switches based on minicomputers. A crucial development was the introduction of a non-terrestrial mode of data traffic through communication satellites. Transnational commercial satellite transmission began in 1965, when the International Satellite Organisation (INTELSAT) launched its first satellite the "Early Bird" on April 6 which became operational as INTELSAT I from June 28, 1965. This satellite had a capacity of 240 two-way audio circuits or one TV channel. Three years later in 1968 a series of INTELSAT II satellites became operational with each having a capacity of 1,500 two-way audio circuits or four TV channels.

With the INTELSAT IV series the capacity became, between 1971 and 1975, 3,750 circuits plus two TV channels. In the 1980s INTELSAT satellites increased their capacity to over 25,000 voice circuits and ten TV channels.

Particularly important for the expansion of world communication is the recent development of mobile satellite communications. This has among others facilitated the emergence of satellite news gathering. Crucial in its development has been the International Maritime Satellite Organisation (Inmarsat) that since 1982 facilitates the telephone, telex, and data communications with ships across the seas and oceans of the world.

A demonstration of mobile satellite communications was Peter Arnett's CNN reporting from the Rashid Hotel in Baghdad. The Gulf War showed to international news media the potential of the Inmarsat system. It set a new pattern of less reliance upon local facilities, but rather on the mobile satellite systems journalists can bring themselves.

The backbone of the mobile satellite system is the Inmarsat-A system with some 2,500 land based and over 11,000 maritime terminals in operation across the world. Inmarsat-A terminals offer a high quality, reliable telephone or telex channel which is easy to operate, 24 hours around the clock.. The portable terminals can also be used for high quality and high speed data transmissions. Inmarsat A can also be used for the increasingly popular telefax transmissions and E-mail network communication. With the latest generation of Inmarsat satellites, Inmarsat-C, world communication is possible with a simple lap-top computer, a light-weight terminal and antenna (3.8 kilo). Inmarsat-C is an advanced packet-data communication system that uses hand-carried low-cost mobile earth stations providing facilities for voice and data communication through satellite or land-lines. Inmarsat and other contenders such as Motorola are actively preparing for the global mobile telephone market that could operate without the cellular networks.

Inmarsat project-21 anticipates a pocket telephone costing less than one thousand dollars and a charge of less than one dollar per minute for use through cellular networks or satellites. In the early 1990s expectations are that by the year 2000 the worldwide mobile satellite community may reach the one or two million users.

Summary

This chapter has described the historical development of world communication. It suggested that although long-distance communication is as old as human history, the specific form of cross-border communication as we know it today originates from the 15th century European news and postal systems. The real growth and significance of world communication began to take shape after the Second World War. The major factors that steered the direction of world communication were East/West and North/South politics, the world economy and its key actors: the transnational corporations, and technological innovations.

Notes

1. The *acta senatus* were the transactions of the Roman Senate and the *acta diurna* were the daily transactions of the Roman people. "The Senate in Rome may have kept a record of its activities . . . as early as 449 B.C. But according to the Roman historian Suetonius, these records were first made public—along with a more general account of political and social life, the *acta diurna*- in 59 B.C. during the first consulship of . . . Julius Caesar . . . . The evidence indicates that news from the acta circulated widely" (Stephens.1988: 66).

2. Source. K.G. Saur (1989). *Yearbook of International Organizations*. Munich.

3. Source. UNESCO (1989). *World Communication Report*. Paris.

4. Source. Salomon Brothers, *Global Telecommunications Review*, 1991.

5. Source. *Business Week*, October 7, 1991: 60.

6. *The Economist* February 29, 1992: 15.

References
Chapple, S. and Garofalo, R. (1977). *Rock 'n Roll is Here to Pay*. Chicago: Nelson Hall.

Hamelink, C.J. (1983). *Finance and Information*. Norwood: Ablex Publishing Corporation.

Hamelink, C.J. (1986). *Militarization in the Information Age*. Geneva: World Council of Churches.

Jasani, B. (1982). (Ed.). *Outer Space -A new dimension of the arms race*. London.

Kunczik, M. (1990).*Images of nations and international public relations*. Bonn: Friedrich Ebert Stiftung.

Pavik, J. V.(1987). *Public Relations: What Research Tells Us*. Newbury Park: Sage.

Tran Van Dinh (1987). *Communication and Diplomacy in A Changing World*. Norwood: Ablex Publishing Corporation.

Smith, A. (1979). *The Newspaper. An International History*. London: Thames and Hudson.

South Commission (1990). *The Challenge to the South. New York*: Oxford University Press.

Stephens, M. (1988). *A History of News*. Harmondsworth: Penguin.

Wilcox, D.L., Ault, Ph., & Age, K. (1989). *Public Relations: Strategies and Tactics. New York:* Harper & Row.

Wright, A.F. (1979). "On the Spread of Buddhism to China". In Lasswell, H.D., Lerner, D. and Speier, H. (Eds.). *Propaganda and Communication in World History.* Volume 1. Honolulu: The University Press of Hawaii.

CHAPTER THREE

Trends in World Communication

In the early 1990s there are important trends observable in the field of world communication that have a considerable impact on the daily lives of people around the world. In this chapter the four most essential current trends and their impact will be discussed. These four major trends originate in the 1980s and mature in the 1990s. They are: digitization, consolidation, deregulation, and globalization.

The four trends are inter-related. They relate to each other both in pro-active and re-active ways. The fundamental trend of digitization, which means that more and more cross-border interactions are based upon electronic formats, reinforces both technological integration and institutional consolidation. These integrated technologies and institutions promote the trend towards deregulated environments and reinforce the trend towards globalization. Also deregulation and globalization are related. Global operations demand global markets which in turn require deregulation of national markets. Digitization provides the technological basis for globalization as it facilitates the global trading of services, worldwide financial networks, and the spreading of high-technology research and development across the globe. Digitization facilitated since the mid-1980s the shift from public to private corporate networks which have become the backbone of global trade. The group of powerful users and operators of corporate global networks has effectively pushed the shift from public to private ownership of telecommunication structures. Consolidation and globalization are related. Consolidation forms the base from which to globalize and also the movement to global markets forces companies to merge in order to remain competitive on a world market.

The Trend Towards Digitization

Digitization means that technologies for the processing and transmission of information have begun to use the same language. This is the computer language of the binary code. This digital language facilitates the convergence of computers, telecommunications, office technologies and assorted audio-visual consumer electronics. This digital integration offers speed, flexibility, reliability, and low costs. Digitization means better technical quality at lower prices. Channels greatly expand their capacity, the Electro Magnetic Spectrum can be more efficiently used, there is more consumer choice and more possibilities for inter-active systems. Economic efficiency is achieved as conversion to digital forms of storage, retrieval, and editing imply savings in time and labour. Digitization considerably improves the quality of voice and video transmission. For high quality video, for example, images can be digitally compressed and then transmitted over satellites as a computer file. The digital data can be stored on computer disc systems before playback in the original speed.

This can be applied in news gathering as available digital compression and storage systems are light-weight. Digital compression techniques in television offer important economic advantages for satellite TV broadcasting. More TV channels can be put on less transponders which means considerable savings. For example, on the Asian satellite AsiaSat the cost of one transponder on an annual basis is US$1.5 million. With digital compression one can get over ten channels on one transponder. This technique will increase the opportunities for projects like video conferencing and pay television.

In the process of digitization earlier analog modes of information transmission and storage began to be replaced by more powerful, reliable, and flexible digital systems. "The technical foundations of this process lay in the early postwar era, in the innovation of a common language of microelectronics for both computing and, somewhat later, telecommunications " (Schiller & Fregoso. 1991:195). As digital switches and digital transmission facilities were developed, increasingly around the world the transition from analog to digital networks began.

As Schiller and Fregoso rightly observe this process does not merely consist of the shifting from analog to digital techniques, but beyond the technical transformation, the process also is institutional—"both in its sources and its implications" (Schiller & Fregoso. 1991: 195). Today's largest users of world communication are demanding broad, affordable, reliable, and flexible electronic highways around the globe. Only a digital global grid can meet these demands. This implies the development of new hardware and software. The digital grid will be expected to transport all signals that can be digitized: from the human voice to High-Definition-TV imagery. This requires the replacement of conventional carriers such as copper wires with optical fibre cables, it means new switches, and new software to control the unprecedented large flows of information across borders. Digital technology makes it possible to send information at the speed of light and at low prices.

In the development of digitization two models have prevailed and collided. The in-house model of corporations that integrate their communications capacities. The insistence of large corporate users that they need their own private networks gave rise to digital systems. The second model originated in the late 1970s as a design by the supplier's side of the telecommunications service industry for ubiquitous integrated systems within and between subscribing nation-states"(Schiller & Fregoso. 1991: 196). This was the ISDN model that moved from domestic telephone networks towards a world-wide connectivity for voice, text, data, and images. The in-house model became the prominent trend. The growing corporate reliance on cross-border information networks made large users to articulate demands for accessing networks world-wide. The drive towards a global grid was of necessity accompanied by an equally strong drive to deregulate communication markets around the globe. Political pressures began building up in many countries to transfer public control over telecommunication institutions to private interests.

Although digital technology has been available since the 1960s, only recently did a strong wave of application, such as Electronic Data Interchange (EDI), emerge that made this technology the essence of more and more cross-border transactions. The "electronification" of cross-border interactions facilitates the provision of a greater variety of services.

Most countries around the world have been affected by the application of digital technologies but perhaps in different ways and at a different pace. During the 1980s the process of digitization began to accelerate and by the late 1980s in the advanced industrial market economies between one-quarter and one-half of all central office telephone switches had been digitized. Actually in the 1980s the international satellite consortium, Intelsat, began to introduce full digital services such as International Business Service (IBS) and Intelnet (digital communications service for use with small terminals). This new commitment to digital technology was seen as essential to Intelsat's future competitiveness on the satellite services market. In the current Intelsat planning the next generation of advanced satellites will be compatible with the standards of integrated digital networks. During the 1980s digital technology began to be applied in consumer electronics and for such products as the compact disc (CD) a rapidly growing market began to emerge. When in 1983 Philips introduced CDs on the Dutch market, sales represented less than 2% of the recorded music market, in 1986 this had risen to over 25%. By 1989 in the USA over 200 million CD units were purchased as compared to some 8 million in 1984 (Robinson, Buck, & Cuthbert. 1991: 53).

The latest in consumer electronics is the innovation of smart digital TV sets. Through the deployment of digital technology HDTV will not only improve sound and image, but also facilitate a series of manipulations with the incoming signals (storing, processing, conversion).

In spite of the expense the deployment of digital technology is not restricted to the rich countries. Early 1992, a six-million dollar advanced digital telephone exchange was commissioned to be installed in Uganda. This new system will link the remote town of Kabale (in South Western Uganda) with the rest of the world. The automatic exchange (with 3,000 lines) is part of a large telecommunications project that links Burundi, Rwanda, Tanzania, and Uganda.[1]

The main feature of digitization is the increasing scale of information-related activities. Information has always been a crucial factor in social processes. Always, people have produced, collected, duplicated, or stolen information. Recent economic and technological developments have, however, significantly changed the scope of these activities. Digitization reinforces a social process in which the production and distribution of information evolves into the most important economic activity in a society, in which information technology begins to function as the key infrastructure for all industrial production and service provision, and in which information itself becomes a commodity tradable on a global scale.

Digital technology is a "synergetic" technology. This means that its growth leads to growth in other sectors of the economy. It creates an infrastructure around its products and services, similar to the car technology earlier in the 20th century. As with the transition from manual power to mechanization techniques and later to electro-mechanical innovations, today's shift towards the pervasive application of electronic information techniques, spawns a scala of new industries, such as software production, processing services, time-sharing facilities, semiconductor manufacturing, database management, or electronic publishing. As a result, issues that in themselves may not be new are confronted with the necessity to find new policy responses as many of the current solutions (in for example criminal law or intellectual property protection) are no longer sufficient. Digitization is largely a response to the demand of the very big users for advanced Digital Information Technology (DIT) applications and DIT-based services.

To meet this demand exceedingly large investments are needed. The investments in digital developments are prohibitively expensive. Prohibitively, that is for most operators except a few very powerful and resource-rich. The risks implied in such enormous investments in a deregulated, competitive environment also are of staggering proportions. Research and Development (R&D) expenses on digital switches between 1984 and 1991 did raise worldwide from US$1 billion to almost US$ 3 billion. This leads to an intensified competition which drives prices per line for digital switches down from an estimated US$300 per line in 1984 to US$225 in 1991.[2] Rising R&D costs and falling prices could be compensated by increases of revenues from the sales of telecommunication equipment (an estimated rise from US$100 billion revenues in 1991 to an estimated US$175 billion in 1998 [3]). One of the inevitable consequences of this configuration will be that only a limited number of firms will survive (this demonstrates the intimate link between the trend of digitization and the trend of consolidation). Large investment in high-risk contexts tends to restrict the market place.

Digitization raises issues of political economy about access, control and expense. Who will have access to the emerging digital grids? And at what price; who can afford? Who will control the networks? Where will the intelligence that guides the network be stored and who will own it? The network operator or the end-user? Who pays the bill for the enormous expense the digital process implies? To digitize the conventional telecommunication structures is enormously expensive.

The potential abuse of DIT and the social consequences are global in nature and require international collaboration and consensus. Unilateral policy measures will not be adequate, as the optimal protection against abuse and optimal benefit from use can only be secured multilaterally.

The impact of digitization will be discussed in the following sections in terms of control and damage.

The Digital Guardians

Digital technology enormously expands the capacity of information capture, processing, and storage. The capacity to handle large volumes of information according to specific detailed requirements of their users has increased dramatically.

A precise tracing of an individual's movements has become possible through the "electronic trace" we leave behind as we use credit cards, rent cars, buy airlines tickets, and purchase items in department stores. The digital age arrives with a monumental invasion of people's privacy. Rapidly increasing volumes of personal information are collected, stored, and sold through vast electronic systems.

Early 1992 a scandal erupted in Spain when the police arrested Joaquin Gonzalez who had built up a very lucrative trade in privacy. His business was buying personal data from a variety of public and private databases and selling them to marketing firms. Gonzales's database had intimate knowledge about which Spanish men had mistresses. His data collection covered 21 million Spanish citizens.

The public sector in many countries has an overwhelming urge to survey its clients. Its claim to provide its services according to the principle of distributive justice justifies the collection of ever large volumes of personal information. As if this is not bad enough, the public sector has also become market oriented and commercialized several of its functions, for instance by selling its information collections to private purchasers. A spectacular plan which was stopped just in time was the 1989 agreement between the Credit Information Services Group of TRW and the Social Security Administration. The plan provided that TRW could compare its credit information file addresses and the social security numbers (SSN) therein with the SSA files, to check whether SSN might have been inaccurate according to SSA files. The plan was to check 140 million SSN for a fee of US$1 million. The Senate Committee hearing in April 1989 revealed that a test had been run on some 150,000 files and similar checks had been run for other companies involving some three million US citizens.

Privacy legislation, which is on the increase around the world, is insufficient since it does not address the basic problem; it leaves the massive collection of data untouched; it does not stop the increasing surveillance of citizens by public and private entities; it only provides you with the right to know that this information is collected and to possibly correct it if it is inaccurate. Against the fact that so much detailed, personal information is collected and that one day a less benign state may abuse this, there is presently no legal protection.

Another example of troubling privacy violation is the proliferation of electronic employee monitoring. This phenomenon encompasses secret video and audiotaping, even in bathrooms, the opening of electronic mail, the use of Video Display Terminals to check employee performance, and the omnipresent telephone bugging. Whatever the excuses or arguments, it amounts to a fundamental violation of human rights. There is little legal protection provided by what could be called the "beep" model of human rights. This refers to the legislation that makes it obligatory to warn employees that their calls are being bugged. The beep signal warns you that from now on your fundamental rights are being violated.

A very recent threat to privacy or what is left of it, concerns biological information. The collection of very sensitive personal information through such diagnostic techniques as genetic screening is becoming a reality. These techniques can generate information about future diseases. Think about the enormous implications this has for the exclusion of high-risk persons from employment or health insurance. The prospect of firms selling genetic profiles to insurers and employers is frightening indeed. Today's human rights legislation provides little or no protection for the biologically under-privileged. In the digital age it is increasingly difficult to know who holds what information on you and for what purposes.

Digital transmission networks require intelligent signalling systems (in order to connect nodes in a network you need data exchange and advanced telecommunication systems which have signalling systems separate from the voice-network that facilitates data communication between the ex-changes). In order to realize or cancel connections between subscribers an exchange of data is needed between subscriber and exchange and between different exchanges. The signalling system creates for all users of the network a Call Detail Record that provides precise information about the pattern of network use by individual subscribers. The development of the Integrated Services Digital Networks in many countries is another area with very complex privacy implications. One of the possibilities of ISDN is automatic caller identification. For example the call can be automatically connected with a computer database. ISDN facilitates the connection be-tween two databases and thus the combination of separate collections of personal data. ISDN facilitates networks through which data banks with name-linked data can be remotely accessed.

Digitization has expanded the range of information-related activities people can engage in while at home: telebanking and teleworking are some examples. This home-telematics opens up another risk of privacy infringement. Very illustrative are the dangers involved in teleworking. "Because the teleworker is beyond the range of the employer's physical supervision, the necessary supervision of the execution of the work will take place via the on-line telecommunication connection with the worker's terminal. Consequently, the worker is subject to the possibility of continuous supervision by an invisible employer. Moreover, the fact that the worker's terminal is located at home means that the employer can also monitor certain aspects of the worker's daily routine" (De Vries. 1990: 202). The market for home-telematics services is international and the multilateral agenda will have to address the concerns about security and privacy protection across borders. It will be necessary to find flexible policy responses that combine constitutional guarantees and forms of industry self-regulation.

The violation of people's private sphere follows the spread of advanced digital technology around the world. Admittedly, people have very different conceptions of privacy. In most Western societies there is a much stronger emphasis on the protected individualistic life than in many Third World societies. Yet, across the globe people know that information about them can be used against them and that surveillance by powerholders is a development to be very suspicious about. Moreover, privacy protection does not only concern individual citizens, it concerns whole nations. Digital technology creates transparent societies, "glass-house" countries that are very vulnerable to external forces and to the loss of their sovereign capacities.

Damage

Digital technology involves risks. If DIT is tampered with airline passengers may die in a crash and patients may be seriously injured, or companies may go bust. The increased technology-dependence and by implication increased vulnerability to technology-failure in many social areas is reinforced by the inherent unreliability of digital computers. Forester and Morrison argue that computers are inherently unreliable as "they are prone to catastrophic failure; and second, their very complexity ensures that they cannot be thoroughly tested before use" (Forester & Morrison. 1990:468). As distinct from analog devices digital systems can suddenly fail totally or behave erratically.

As digital systems are discrete state devices, they can be in an infinite number of states and the execution of each state depends upon the earlier state to be correct. The magnitude of possible disruptions is mind-boggling. Software bugs, systems malfunction, computer crime and hacking can cost millions of dollars and human lives. Computer software errors may cause over-billing, false arrest, but also loss of life and grave injury. When in November 1988 a computer virus disrupted the US nationwide ARPANET computer system this forced some 6,000 computers to be shut down for two days leading to a total damage of over US$99 million (Russo, Hale, & Helm. 1989: 4-13). (*New York Times*, November 13, 1988, B-1). The Michelangelo virus of early March 1992 did not create as much damage as it could have since there was timely warning across the world. Several reports did mention however that some 10,000 computers had been hit worldwide. The virus did wipe out contents of hard disks of the infected computers.

A telling illustration of very real damage is the case of a Nevada women, a Ms. Julie Engle. Ms. Engle underwent routine surgery in hospital. The operation was completed without complication. However, soon afterward Ms. Engle was administered pain relief by a computerized dispensing machine. Unfortunately, the system mistakenly instructed hospital staff to pump more than 500 mg of pain-relieving drugs into Ms. Engle's body and within 390 minutes of the successful completion of the operation, she was found to be in a coma. Five days later, she was pronounced brain dead. A damages suit was launched for incorrect and irresponsible use of an expert system.[4] Somewhat similar cases occurred in 1986 when in Texas through computer malfunction lethal overdoses of radiation were given to cancer patients.

An obvious manifestation of security concerns is the possibility, and increasingly the reality, of computer abuse for criminal purposes. Several highly publicized cases in the late 1980s (such as illegal access to computer systems in Canada from New York or unauthorised access to NATO information systems in Norway from the USA) have shown that "the prevention of computer crime is of great significance as business, administration and society depend to a high degree on the efficiency and security of modern information technology". (Sieber. 1990: 119).

Among some of the earlier signals that pointed at the problem of technology-vulnerability is the 1978 report by the Swedish Ministry of Defence Committee on the Vulnerability of Computer Systems (SARK) entitled "The Vulnerability of Computerized Society". In 1981 the Organization for Cooperation and Economic Development (OECD) held a workshop in Sigüenza (Spain) on the vulnerability of the Computerized Society. In 1984 the American Federation of Information Processing Societies published a report on the matter and in the same year the Information Task Force of the Commission of the European Communities published "The vulnerability of the information-conscious society-European situation." In 1986 the Norwegian Vulnerability Commission presented a report called "The Vulnerability of a Computer Dependent Society". In 1989 a committee of the British Computer Society reported that current skills in safety assessment were inadequate and therefore the safety of people could not be guaranteed.

In a very broad sense the introduction of vulnerable and fallible technological systems does raise the question of accountability for technology choice and its potentially negative impact. The introduction of ISDN in Europe provides an interesting case. This is the largest European public project (amounting to over 20 million ECU) implemented without any public consultation; the main driving force is technology opportunity; the major concern is with error cost (the cost of not having it) rather than with the potential social cost; there is no vision for a social policy on such questions as non-discriminatory tariffing or protection against cultural erosion.

The ISDN project is a major exercise in flying blind toward a sophisticated and expensive highway system with no idea as to who will ride the roads, at what price, and with how many traffic accidents. The majority of European countries is intent on implementing ISDN plans irrespective of warnings that it is the "Concorde of the European telecommunications industry" and that the acronym stands for Innovations Subscribers Don't Need. So far there has been little litigation in the courts on malfunctioning information technologies. The proliferation and increasing dependency on these technologies could indeed mean that providers of information-based services are increasingly faced with complainants who experienced damage. An issue to address is whether the rule adopted in most national courts that providers of mass media services are not held liable for inaccurate information, will also be applied in cases of computerized information dissemination through international networks.

Digital technology creates particularly for the less powerful users dangerous levels of vulnerability to external control. Herewith, the political and economic security of countries and their citizens are at stake. The rapidly increasing scope of information provision around the world thanks to digital technology, confronts more and more people with a dependence upon data that may be incomplete by intent or default. If people's lives are affected by such data in very negative ways, there is little they can do about it.

The Trends Towards Consolidation

As all signals, whether they carry sound, data, or pictures, converge into the digital format, they become, however different in substance, identical in the technical sense. As a result, telecommunication and broadcasting integrate, i.e. telecommunication services can be provided by TV cable networks or TV signals can be carried by telecommunication operators. This raises complex regulatory problems (what kind of legislation) and institutional issues (what kind of jurisdiction), and also consumer questions about the quality of services on offer. Although to-day it is still feasible to distinguish computer manufacturers, telephone service companies, publishing houses, broadcasters, and film producers as separate industrial actors, they are rapidly converging into one industrial activity.

The technical convergence leads to institutional convergence and to the consolidation of national and international provision of information (and culture) into the hands of a few mega-providers. To remain competitive in world communication, companies need to bring formerly separate faculties under one roof. AT&T, for example, is doing just that. As AT&T CEO Bob Allen believes, the company can be a global information power house by putting together a set of resources that no other company can match: a sophisticated worldwide network to carry voice and data, plus the equipment to run it, plus the devices that hook up to it, from Mickey Mouse phones to laptop computers.[5]

The early 1990s are already christened the Age of Consolidation. "Everywhere you look these days, archrivals are falling into each other's embrace".[6] Megamergers in both manufacturing and services sectors are emerging. The US economy in particular provides stark illustrations in such sectors as banking and aviation. Consolidation basically means that companies are buying their competitors and thus concentrating market control in the hands of fewer companies. *Business Week* made this comment on megamergers: "It was inaugurated during the dealmaking 1980s, which left airlines, tires, and appliances in the hands of virtual cartels. And it's being propelled by ferocious foreign competition, a sluggish and capacity-glutted U.S. economy, and swelling research-and-development costs. Now, the wave is rolling into fresh sectors of the economy—banking, insurance, pharmaceuticals, retailing, commercial real estate. It's even touching youthful industries such as software and biotechnology".[7] The complex policy problem is that for global competitiveness consolidation may be necessary, the risk exists however that domestically it restricts the level of competition that may be good for consumers and product and service quality. A crucial problem is evidently whether the global conglomerates will use their market power to "price-gouge consumers". It may well be that in the initial stages of consolidation prices (e.g. for airline tickets) go down, but once the market is settled, there is a strong likelihood of rapidly increasing costs to consumers.

The age of consolidation has also arrived for the communication sector. In all the segments of the communication market there are observable trends towards a high rate of concentration and all indications are that this will continue throughout the 1990s. Throughout the 1980s important alliances have been established between actors in the transnational information industry. In the hardware sector of the industry alliances have developed between, for example:

- CGE (France) and ITT (USA);
- Sony (Japan) and AT&T (USA);
- Philips (the Netherlands) and Matsushita (Japan);
- IBM (USA) and Ericsson (Sweden);
- Philips (the Netherlands) and AT&T (USA);
- Ericsson (Sweden) and Thorn-EMI (Great Britain).
- Apple (USA) and Toshiba (Japan).

Illustrations of alliances in the media sector were:

- The cooperation between Maxwell and Berlusconi in TV news programme production;
- Murdoch and Maxwell announced in 1989 (May 16) an agreement between Murdoch's Sky Television satellite operation and the Maxwell Cable Television company.
- The Walt Disney concern and News International (Rupert Murdoch) have established a joint company for their TV products;
- General Occidentale (publisher of *L'Express*) has begun cooperation with Bertelsmann in the bookclub France Loisirs;
- February 21 1990; four companies announced the launch of a consortium for a high power direct broadcast satellite service beginning in 1993. The partners are: Hughes Communications Inc., National Broadcasting Co., Cablevisions Systems Corp., and News Corp. Ltd.

Mergers have also developed across hardware and software interests, such as in the case of Sony purchasing Columbia Pictures and CBS Records or Matsushita acquiring MCA and Universal Pictures. Interesting forms of across-industry collaboration did emerge, such as between IBM and NBC in the provision of computerized TV news. Very active in the creation of networks between multimedia interests and hardware manufacturers is the combination Time-Warner with the recently developing ties with companies such as Toshiba and AT&T.

Market analysts expect that by the year 2000 only few telecommunication megacompanies will control global network services.

"From around 10 diversified equipment makers now competing internationally, perhaps five or six will survive as global rivals with a full range of products by the turn of the century".[8] Leaders are expected to be AT&T, Northern Telecom Ltd., Siemens, Alcatel, Ericsson, NEC Corp. and Fujitsu Ltd. The telecommunication business has spent in the second half of the 1980s over US$5 billion in mergers and acquisitions.

Also in international advertising the trend is towards the creation of megacompanies. The ten largest advertising agencies in the world are owned by only four conglomerates. These are WPP (UK), Saatchi & Saatchi (UK), Interpublic (USA) and Omnicom (USA). Their worldwide billings are given in Table 8.

In the music industry the four largest companies account for over 73% of the world market. These companies, Thorn/EMI, Polygram, Warner and Sony, practically control with two other major firms, Bertelsmann and Matsushita, the total market. (see Table 9).

At the same time, the international news market is developing a strong trend towards consolidation. For printed news there are on the world market (after the sales of UPI to Middle East Broadcasting), only Associated Press, Reuters, and Agence France Press. For visual news there are two leading agencies the former Visnews, now Reuters Television, and World Television Network. Reuters TV supplies TV news to over 400 broadcasters in 85 countries reaching almost a half-billion households. WTN provides to 200 broadcasters in 85 countries has an audience of some three billion people. In 1993 there were serious speculations that Reuter was planning to acquire WTN thus reducing the two major players to one market leader.

TABLE 8. *Agency (and agencies included) 1990 Billings in US$million.*

1. WPP (UK)
   Ogilvy&Mather, J Walter Thompson   18,09

2. Saatchi&Saatchi (U.K.)
   Backer, Spielvogel, Bates   11,86

3. Interpublic (USA)
   McCann-Erikson, Lintas   11,02

4. Omnicom (USA)
   BBDO, DDB, Needham   9,70

5. Dentsu (Japan)   9,672

6. Young & Rubicam (USA)   8,001

7. Eurocom (France)   5,066

Source: *Advertising Age*, March 25, 1991.

Second in line for international TV news production and distribution are BBC World Service and CNN. The BBC started a 24-hours TV news service for Asia in 1991. Through AsiaSat BBC's Worldservice Television reaches to 38 countries with a potential audience of almost 3 billion viewers. CNN distributes around the clock to over 200 subscribers. Per average day some 160 items are broadcast of which about 30 are international. CNN is available in some 100 million households worldwide and thousands of hotels. In the course of 1993 the news agency Associated Press announced that it was ready to enter the TV news market in early 1994. APTV would probably be the most serious competitor for Reuters Television and WTN.

While the megacompanies were still struggling to justify their merger activities of the 1980s, a series of new megadeals were underway in 1993. Ted Turner (CNN) began to talk to Time-Warner and made plans for a merger of his film company MGM with the other 'major' Paramount and the TV network ABC. The computer firm Apple considered a bid for broadcasting company NBC. The most striking battle developed around Paramount

Pictures—the only remaining independent Hollywood company—in September 1993. On September 13, Paramount and Viacom Inc. announced a US$8.2 billion merger into Paramount Viacom International. The new company is expected to enjoy an annual revenues of US$ 6.2 billion and thus become the fifth largest mediaconglomerate on the world market.

TABLE 9. *Recorded Music Companies in 1991 Market Shares Labels.*

COMPANY	SHARE	LABELS
Thorn/EMI	20.0%	EMI Records, Capitol, Chrysalis, SBK
Polygram	18.5%	Polydor, Islands, A&M
Warner	18.5%	Atlantic, Elektra, Sire, Warner
Sony	16.5%	CBS, Epic, Def Jam
Bertelsmann	n.a.	Arista, RCA
Matsushita	n.a.	MCA, Geffen, Motown

Viacom is the cable and TV station empire of Sumner Redstone (who owns 76% of the Viacom stock) that operates MTV and the children's channel Nickelodeon. In 1992 Viacom profits reached almost US$50 million. Paramount owns the Paramount film and TV business and also publishers Simon & Schuster, Prentice Hall, and Pocket Books. The greatest asset of Paramount is likely to be its huge movie library of over 900 films with such titles as *The Godfather, Indiana Jones, Star Trek, Beverly Hills Cops* and *The Firm.* In 1992 Paramount showed a profit of over US$260 million. The Viacom-Paramount deal was contested by QVC Network Inc. that offered US$ 9.5 billion in stock and cash. As the battle heated up other contenders got involved and among them were Ted Turner and Time-Warner. Early November 1993 Viacom increased its own initial bid for Paramount to the US$10 billion mark. Also in November, Paramount announced that it had acquired the most prestigious company in the former Maxwell empire, MacMillan publishing for US$552.8 million. MacMillan is now part of Paramount Publishing, the largest publishing house in the USA. In December 1993 Paramount accepted the bid made by QVC and this looked like the end of the battle. However, in early 1994 Viacom merged with Blockbuster, a leading chain of music and videoshops in the USA. At the time of this writing it is unclear whether the new company will offer Paramount a deal that outbids QVC. On October 13, 1993 the largest communications merger in US history was announced: the megadeal between Bell Atlantic and Telecommunications Inc. The deal implied the acquisition by regional phone company Bell Atlantic (with 1992 operating revenues of US$12.6 billion) of cable operator TCI (with 1992 operating revenues of US$3.6 billion). This merger of a large phone company (with over 18 million phone lines) and the largest US owner and operator of cable systems (with over 13 million subscribers) will redesign the vast cable network for telephone service and make the phone network into a vast video conveyor belt. The new company can offer the whole spectre of communication services ranging from video phone calls to movies on demand and telemedicine. James H. Quello, chairman of the US Federal Communications Commission called the Bell Atlantic-TCI merger, "the most momentous deal of the decade in a decade of huge mergers, acquisitions and joint ventures".[9]

The current wave of mergers in the communication industry is different from earlier processes of concentration. Today's oligopolisation is caused by very large and profitable companies that merge into mega-companies (See table 10), whereas before (for example in the 1960s) concentration usually meant that big companies acquired small, loss-making firms.

Among the key factors that explain consolidation are the following:

1. The past years have seen a considerable increase of the scale at which communication markets operate. As a result it has become necessary for many companies to combine the production and distribution of hardware products with the related software. As Michael Schulhof, President of Sony USA, observes, "unless you have software to support your hardware, you can't have a successful industry".[10]

2. In order for companies to operate competitively on global markets, they need to achieve dominance on domestic markets and thus shake-out domestic competitors.

3. In the past years some sectors of the industry, such as the publishing houses, have been particularly profitable, and had to find investments for their surplus cash. Acquiring competing companies seemed an attractive strategy.

4. In some cases (for example the Time-Warner merger) a mega-merger appeared to be the only solution to foreign competition (in this case Bertelsmann) in the home-market.

TABLE 10. *The World's Top Twenty Media and Entertainment Companies in 1992.*

COMPANY	COUNTRY	SALES 1992 (IN US$ BILLION)
Time-Warner	USA	13.0
Matra-Hachette	France	10.4
Bertelsmann	Germany	9.7
Walt Disney	USA	7.5
News Corp.	Australia	6,9
Thorn-EMI	UK	6,4
Capital Cities/ABC	USA	5,3
Havas	France	5,2
Sony Entertainment*	Japan	5,0
Paramount	USA	4,3
Rank Organisation	UK	3,8
Elsevier	Netherlands	3,8
Polygram	Netherlands	3,7
CBS	USA	3,5
Matsushita Entertainment*	Japan	3,3
Pearson	UK	2,5
Reuters	UK	2,4
McGraw-Hill	USA	2,0
Viacom	USA	1,9
Turner Broadcasting	USA	1,8

* sales for 1991

The emerging mega-industries combine programme production (ranging from digital libraries to TV entertainment), the manufacturing and operating of distribution systems (ranging from satellites to digital switches), and building the equipment for reception and processing of information (ranging from HDTV-sets to telephones). As the consolidation trend shows companies are actively trying to get control over at least two of these three components. One example is the Japanese company Sony that was already active in the equipment sector when it acquired through Columbia Pictures and CBS-records access to the programming component. The following figures show the economic significance of the world's leading mega media companies:

The Berlusconi Group. In the early 1990s the Berlusconi Group was gaining increased control over European TV markets, Sylvio Berlusconi was en route to becoming Europe's media kingpin. One of Europe's largest advertising companies Publitalia '80 belongs to the Berlusconi group. The Group produces films on a large-scale with the Leo Kirch Group of Germany and TF1 from France. The Berlusconi company has also established a production company in Hollywood and holds a vast library of over 100,000 TV hours as well as exclusive European distribution rights to programmes such as *Twin Peaks, Dallas* and *Dynasty*.

Bertelsmann. In 1990 Bertelsmann was filled with cash for expansion. It had only some US\$300 million total debt (compared to some US\$10.8 billion debt Time-Warner has resulting from its 1989 merger; or Murdoch's US\$2.2 billion debt) and over US\$2 billion for investments. The company had announced a budget for the 1990/1993 period of some US\$4 billion for international expansion. It spent over US\$600million just to win control of the former East German information market.[11]

DISTRIBUTION OF BERTELSMANN REVENUES:

Publishing/ Book Clubs:	US\$3.3 billion
Records/CDs/Music Videos:	US\$2.1 billion

Magazines/Newspapers: US$2.0 billion

Printing: US$1.7 billion

TV Production/Broadcasting: US$0.5 billion

Matsushita/MCA. "Electronics giant Matsushita, anxious to secure a ready supply of movies and TV shows for its video recorders and high-definition TV sets, had watched archrival Sony Corp. snap up CPE in 1989, reducing to three the number of major independent studios. MCA, unnerved at the spiralling costs of making movies and building theme parks, long had been casting about for a deep-pocketed partner. But the pressure intensified as Time Inc. bought Warner Communications Inc. and MCA found itself dwarfed by global giants". Matsushita was advised by Oviz's Creative Artists Agency (who had found CPE for Sony) to purchase MCA "because of its huge film library and its growing record business".[12] The deal was closed for US$6 billion.

DISTRIBUTION OF MATSUSHITA/MCA REVENUES:

Filmed entertainment: US$1.7 billion

Music: US$765 million

Book Publishing: US$189 million

Other incl., TV station):   US$690 million

MTV. This leading music television station (with close to US$2 billion revenue) is owned largely by tycoon Sumner Redstone (who also owns MTV's parent Viacom). It beams its signals into over 200 million households in over 70 countries. By comparison although Ted Turner's CNN is received in over 130 countries, it reaches only some 100 million households. Also MTV revenues are growing faster than those of CNN. In the past five years MTV has rapidly expanded into Europe, Australia, Latin America, Russia, and Asia. Together with the global consolidation of MTV, Redstone is planning to introduce the popular children's channel Nickelodeon, also owned by Viacom, to non-US markets. This is being done through co-production arrangements with local companies, such as Canal Plus in France.

DISTRIBUTION OF **MTV** REVENUES:

MTV & VH-1:	US$243 million
Nickelodeon:	US$169 million
Showtime :	US$501 million
Entertainment :	US$271 million
Cable systems:	US$378 million
Broadcasting:	US$159 million[13]

Murdoch's News Corp. The company received a total revenue of US$7.2 billion with an operating income of US$1.1 billion.[14]

DISTRIBUTION OF NEWS CORP. REVENUES.

Newspapers:	US$535 million
Magazines:	US$244 million
Television:	US$6.3 million
Movies:	US$82 million

Sony Corp. Sony purchased CBS Records Inc. for US$2 billion in 1988 and Columbia Pictures Entertainment Inc. for US$3.4 billion in 1989. Revenues by March 1991 were some US$5 billion in movies, (Columbia and Tri-Star Pictures), Television (Columbia Pictures TV), and Music (Sony Music Entertainment).

DISTRIBUTION OF SONY REVENUES:

TV & advertising:	US$2 billion
Publishing:	US$1.5 billion
Retailing:	US$3.2 billion.

Impact

The impact of these mega-mergers can be discussed in terms of access to information, quality and diversity of information provision and the variety of cultural production. Oligopolization in the communication industry tends to undermine the civil and political fundamental right to freedom of expression. This is the case when concentration actually diminishes the number of channels that citizens can use to express or receive opinions. In oligopolistic markets it becomes easier for the controlling interests to refuse the distribution of certain opinions. It is also easier in such situations, for example, to refuse certain forms of advertisement. For oligopolists there is always the tendency to use their market power to "price-gouge" consumers. This may easily mean that the access to information and culture becomes dependent upon the level of disposable income. The key question is whether consolidation does create adequate structural conditions for effective communication freedom. Communication freedom would seem to demand a large variety of autonomous media, a diversity of owners, and many channels accessible to the public. Research on concentration tends to focus on the issue of content and the effects of media concentration in performance and then conclude that it is "very difficult to demonstrate any link between the two" (McQuail. 1992: 125). This may be so, but the media-performance (in the sense of contents) is hardly the core issue.

What is more relevant are the questions on whether consolidation guarantees sufficient independent locations for media workers, does it guarantee enough channels for audience reception and/or access, does it provide adequate protection against price controls on oligopolistic markets, does it permit newcomers on markets? Even if the oligopolist demonstrates quality, fairness, diversity, critical debate, objectivity, investigative reporting, resistance to external pressures in his offerings to the market place, there will remain the need to provide regulatory correction as the market place will effectively be closed to newcomers and thus not constitute a free market. An important dimension of communication freedom is the level of independence in information provision and cultural production.

Industrial concentration inevitably implies the establishment of power. The mega-companies are centres of power that are at the same time subject and object of media exposure. Moreover, the information industry as power centre is linked into other circuits of power, such as the financial institutions, the military establishments, and the political elite.

A problem arises when the mass media that provide news and commentary are part of an industrial conglomerate. The conglomerate may engage in activities that call for critical scrutiny by the media but which the controlling actors prefer to protect against exposure. The close interlocks between the US media and the military contractors may have contributed to the partisan way in which the Gulf War was reported.

The National Broadcasting Corporation (one of the three leading US networks) is owned by General Electric. "As it turns out, GE designed, manufactured or supplied parts or maintenance for nearly every important weapons system employed by the USA during the Gulf War, including the much-praised Patriot and Tomahawk Cruise missiles, the Stealth bomber, the B-52 bomber, the AWACS plane, the Apache and Cobra helicopters and the NAVSTAR spy satellite system. Few TV viewers in the USA were aware of the inherent conflict of interest whenever NBC correspondents and commentators praised the performance of US weapons. In nearly every instance, they were extolling equipment made by GE, the corporation that pays their salaries" (Lee. 1991: 29.). As a former NBC employee observed, "The whole notion of freedom of the press becomes a contradiction when the people who own the media are the people who need to be reported on" (Lee. 1991: 29).

It could be argued that the core of a democratic society is the presence of a public debate about the distribution and execution of power. It is crucial for democratic arrangements that choices made by the power holders are publicly scrutinized and contested. In the public debate the informational and cultural products play a significant role. If the interests of the information and culture producers and the powers that be are intertwined, a society's capacity for democratic government is seriously undermined. In the trend toward consolidation people's access to independent information sources and their access to a diversity of channels for the expression of their opinions is under serious threat.

Diversity

It should be noted that diversity is meant here in a wider sense than the conventional notion of democratic pluralism or economic liberalism. It refers here to a broad standard that among others encompasses the access of a wide range of actors to world communication. This was one of the

paramount concerns in the 1970s debates on a new international information order. Oligopolization can threaten to erode the diversity of informational and cultural production. However, this is not always the case. It can
be attractive for the oligopolist to bring competing products on the market.
We see this happening quite commonly in such sectors as cosmetics or
detergents. This intra-firm diversity helps to erect very effective obstacles
against the market-entry of newcomers. This is important since market
diversity frequently originates with new entrants.

It is also true that large firms may support loss-making operations by
compensating the losses elsewhere in the company accounts. In this way
newspapers, for example, that otherwise would have disappeared can be
maintained. However, the length of time this compensation will be acceptable to shareholders (and in particular institutional investors) is limited.
Moreover, losses accumulate over time and in the middle-to longer term
products that are not profitable will have to be removed.

In cases where consolidation occurs as vertical integration, meaning that
production and distribution are controlled by the same actors, the real
danger exists that they will exclusively offer their own products to the
market. A common example is the newspaper that as part of a conglomerate
publishes mainly reviews of its own books. The growing influence of
institutional investors and commercial interests not genuine to the information sector tends to lead to an emphasis on the profitability of the commodity, rather than on its socio-cultural quality. As a result there is a preference
for products that can be rapidly sold on mass markets. Illustrative of this is
the tendency among film production companies and recorded music producers to concentrate on "blockbusters". This "Rambo" and "Madonna"
tendency reinforces a homogenization of markets as the less profitable
products are avoided. It should be realized at this point that even if
regulatory measures against industrial consolidation would be successful in
stimulating more competition, there would be no guarantee of more product diversity. Markets tend inevitably towards identical, though marginally
distinct, products since they address by necessity the largest possible
number of buyers .

Allowing competition on the marketplace does not necessarily lead to more diversity. There is some evidence that the deregulated, competitive broadcast systems of West European countries reflect less diversity in contents than the formerly regulated, public monopolies. This is largely due to the fact that on a competitive market the actors all try to control the largest segment by catering to rather similar tastes and preferences of that market segment.

The limits to diversity are also defined by the common frame that media adopt for their coverage of international and national events. This may allow for a wide range of shades of opinion, but not for a fundamental dissidence. Ample evidence of the presence of a common frame could be found during the Cold War years. Media from progressive to conservative would differ on many things, but not on the common frame of a liberal, democratic, capitalist social arrangement as basic to the societies of the West. Social issues would not normally be analysed from a totally different frame, for example that of a communist, non-market economy type of arrangement.

The Trend Towards Deregulation

The trends towards digitization and consolidation go together with a shift from regulated, controlled public-service type information and telecommunication services to a competitive environment for the trading of these services by private market operators. At the same time the trend towards deregulation strongly reinforces both digitization and consolidation.

In response to recent economic and technological developments many countries around the world are revising their communication and information structures. In this process the leading stratagem would seem to be "more market, less state" and the buzzwords have become privatization and liberalization. Whereas privatization refers to the complete sale of publicly owned companies to private interests as well as abolishing regulations that prevent private entrepreneurs from going into certain economic sectors, liberalization refers to a de-monopolization of markets by introducing competition in the supply of information and telecommunication services. Privatization and liberalization have occured in telecommunications, public libraries and public data banks. Deregulation became the key policy orientation of the 1980s. This decade was characterized by a wave of telecommunications deregulation finding concrete expression in privatization and liberalization. In fact, the concept is somewhat misleading as deregulation tends to mean re-regulation and often leads to rather more than less rules. Deregulation also tends to refer to the withdrawal of the state from very special social areas. There is a trend in many countries to dispense with state involvement in the area of social welfare. At the same time one observes in the same countries increased state involvement and related regulation in the fields of technology policy and industrial policy.

Also in the politics of communication the dominant ideology is the old Adam Smith superstition that a free market would be to the benefit of everybody. However, a free market under capitalist conditions leads inevitably to a concentration of capital, growth of transnational corporations, and forms of industrial oligopolization which are not necessarily supportive of everybody's interest and need. The first period of privatization commenced in the late 1950s within the USA. As telecommunication users "became aware of their growing dependence on telecommunications, they organized to lobby government authorities for specific, far-reaching change in the rules governing domestic telecommunications provisions" (Schiller & Fregoso. 1991: 198). By and large the telecommunication regulators affirmed business users' demands. In the 1980s telecommunications systems in the USA, UK and Japan shifted to deregulatory policies. On January 1, 1984 the mega-telecommunication operator AT&T was broken up into its 22 local companies. In exchange AT&T was now at liberty to enter new types of business. In 1985 the sale of 51% of Britain's nationally owned British Telecom shares to private sector interests was authorized by the UK government.

Also in 1985 Japan developed a new policy towards the liberalization of its telecommunications operations. The largest operator Nippon Telephone & Telegraph lost its monopoly in exchange for the permission to begin new competitive lines of communication business. Part of the government's ownership of NT&T was sold to the private sector and new local voice carriers were allowed in the market place. With the development of transnational data networks and the growth of transborder data flows, the trend towards deregulation is exported from core to periphery countries and this raises the question about the adequacy of globalizing a policy that originates in a specific historical context to all countries at the same time.

Impact

The impact of deregulation will be discussed in terms of universal service, market access, and commercialization.

Universal Service. Are privatization and liberalization compatible with universal service? This question needs to be addressed as the standard of universal service has been essential to the provision of telecommunication services from their inception. For example the US 1934 Communications Act demands "to make available, so far as possible, to all people of the United States, a rapid, efficient, nationwide and worldwide wire and radio communications service with adequate facilities at reasonable charges". What will happen to universal service in the competitive battle between private entrepreneurs? Given the levels of expenditure will private entrepreneurs continue to meet public obligations of universal service, universal accessibility? Will there be a commercial incentive to narrow the information capacity disparity within and between nations? What will happen to telecommunication tariffs for residential use if with the lowering of international charges the cross-subsidization of local calls stops? What happens if competition on crowded traffic routes, such as the transatlantic route leads to capacity glut on dense routes and what are the implications for the thin routes. Could "cream-skimming" make the operating of thin routes less feasible?

The pressures that create world competitiveness have an impact on national pricing policies. They cause a tendency to base telecommunication tariffs on a cost-based system (e.g. in Germany) which raises serious problems for the conventional cross-subsidization of residential users with excess charges on large business users. The adoption of new pricing policies may lead public service ideals into grave jeopardy.

By and large universal service (through these different interpretations) has been based on different patterns of cross-subsidization as pricing strategy.

"Under liberalization cost-based pricing involves a reduction in long-distance tariffs, an increase in local call charges and an increase in the charges levied on individual subscribers (these subscribers being once again made responsible for meeting the cost of the local loop" (Hills, J. 1989: 134). The liberalization argument continues by stating that "if individual subscribers are too poor to meet the increased costs of access then they must forfeit telephone service and drop off the network. If governments wish the network to be 'universal' then they must pay a subsidy to have these people kept on" (Hills, J. 1989: 134). Although there is not sufficient strong evidence on large numbers of subscribers being forced off the network, there is evidence that privatization and liberalization have not increased the penetration of telephone networks. This is largely due to the fact that deregulation tends to increase costs of connection, rental and usage. "In the USA consumer groups argue that the divestiture of AT&T has disenfranchised groups of consumers from use of the telephone by the rebalancing of charges and the liberalization of the local network monopoly—these groups are the elderly, the poor and those living in high-cost rural areas" (Hills, J. 1989: 139). There are a number of initiatives developed to address this, such as subsidization schemes. However, consumer groups argue that these emergency measures are not adequate. They provide access to the emergency box, but this does not constitute universal service. "The argument adopted by consumer groups in the USA is that access is not universal service—that the telephone should be priced at a level which makes it possible for disadvantaged groups to use it for social reasons rather than simply as an emergency service" (Hills. 1989: 141). The data on penetration in the USA suggest that since the AT&T divestiture national telephone penetration has not decreased. (Fuhr. 1990: 187), but this may be different for actual usage.

"Consumer groups claim that usage of the telephone has decreased among lower-income groups, such as the elderly. The American Association of Retired Persons argues that one in five people over the age of 55 years have had to reduce their telephone usage" (Hills, J. 1989: 142).

The international ramifications of deregulatory policies have emerged quite clearly in the context of the services provided by international satellite operators. Although opinions are divided on this, there has been since the beginning of Intelsat operations a level of cross-subsidization. "Intelsat is currently responsible for the delivery of approximately 70% of the world's international telephone calls and virtually all international television transmission. Since its very beginning Intelsat has enjoyed a near monopoly status in the delivery of satellite communications. Through an economic policy of global price averaging, Intelsat has ensured affordable communications on a worldwide basis. To accomplish this, Intelsat takes revenues derived from high-traffic routes (e.g. the North Atlantic region, USA to Europe) and subsidizes the less profitable traffic routes that interconnect geographically isolated and/or developing nations" (Gershon. 1990: 249).

By the mid-1980s a number of applications for the provision of satellite services had been received by the US Federal Communications Commission. Applicants were Orion Satellite Corporation (March 1983), International Satellite Inc (August 1983), RCA (February 1984), Cygnus Corporation (March 1984) and Pan American Satellite Inc (May 1984). Only the PanAmSat application asked authorization for international carrier services between the USA and Latin America. The others were only interested in the provision of private satellite services (information traffic within a network owned or leased by the customer) in the North American region. Intelsat clearly began to feel uneasy about the prospect of cream-skimming competitors. In 1985 the then Intelsat Director General Richard R. Colino wrote "While deregulation and free-market competition are suitable in some business environments, in others they can cause ruinous failures with devastating social implications if not carefully and effectively managed" (Gershon. 1990: 252). In November 1984 the Reagan administration launched its "Open Skies" policy that would promote international competition in telecommunications as well as maintain the viability of Intelsat. If Intelsat will have to compete with other satellite operators, but also increasingly with fibre optic cable operators that will apply high-density routes based pricing systems, will the integrated global pricing system of Intelsat survive? (Gershon. 1990: 249) If deregulatory policies would indeed threaten universal service then even less people than to-day have access to ways of communicating with each other.

Market Access. What will the impact upon developing country markets be if the international trade negotiations in such fora as the GATT will indeed reinforce a worldwide deregulatory environment?

What are the effects of deregulatory policies on infant service industries in Third World countries, and what are the consequences of global open markets for local cultural production? Will trade liberalization benefit those countries that have large trade deficits in services?

With the costs of telecommunications going down, one can expect a rapid growth of information-based services that are supplied by telecommunication-based delivery systems. Such services run around the world into national regulatory obstacles and the resolution of concerns about international trade barriers is high on the political agenda. Regulation of service activities is often closely related to specific national goals. This is evident in such cases as the regulation of banking and insurance and the operations of airlines and telecommunications. Here considerations of national security or public interest have an import on regulatory measures. A principal question is when are national rules reasonable, and when do they constitute protectionism? Discrimination against foreign suppliers may be considered inappropriate and protectionist. However, particular countries may intentionally discriminate foreign suppliers of cultural goods (films/television programmes/advertising) that can be seen as eroding their cultural identity.

It may also be that national policy makers want to tie foreign service providers to rules related to transfer of technology or local employment markets. The policy challenge will be to find the equilibrium between the legitimate domestic concerns of national governments and the free trade rules of the multilateral arrangement that emerged from GATT negotiations.

Particularly for the developing countries the key question is how to benefit from present shifts in the international regulatory environment and how to protect their interests in a liberal, competitive market. This raises issues such as what levels of freedom shall be granted to global entrepreneurs to access foreign markets using telecommunication systems for the delivery of their services, attaching customized equipment to local networks, leasing telecommunication lines and/or the implementation of private networks.

Crucial concepts in recent negotiations on traded services were "market access", "right of permanent establishment", and "national treatment". The combined effect of such norms rules out any local protection of domestic service industries, inhibits the development of indigenous service industries, and diminishes local control over key service industries. Once one realizes that among such industries are the mass media, telecommunication services, advertising, marketing, and tourism, it becomes clear that the application of these norms reduces local cultural autonomy. Local cultural markets are monopolized by transnational corporations that leave little space for local cultural providers. Liberalizing world trade to the extent that smaller and less resource-rich countries open their services markets to outsiders, stimulates the development of consumerist lifestyles and erodes the competitive capacity of people's own cultural industries.

Commercialization . A deregulatory environment that facilitates transactions of information may also facilitate the commercialization of culture. This is because information and culture tend to become identified as commercial services subject to classical trade rules. In this connection the decision of the European Commission to define broadcasting as 'service' and thus apply the competition rules of the EEC Treaty to this commercial activity is a telling illustration. The ensuing tension between public good and private commodity is increasingly resolved to the latter's advantage.

Commercialization implies that increasingly citizens are required to pay for information services rendered by public bodies. In many countries governmental departments charge for information that is generated through public finance, they levy fees for the use of data collections or sell these through private on-line service operators. Whereas the trend towards digitization facilitates an unprecedented access to information, there is a good chance that deregulatory policies that reinforce commercialization would relate this access to the affordability of the service. Commercialization implies that price and not public interest is the decisive factor. This may lead to the peculiar phenomenon of more and more people disconnecting from the "information society" as they can no longer afford the charges.

Commercialization also implies the erosion of the public sphere. Since the early 1980s a process has begun that increasingly erodes the public sphere in many societies through the penetration of corporate interests into terrains formerly protected by public interest, such as government information, public libraries, or the arts. Commercial sponsoring of more and more socio-cultural activities has become very popular and leads to the emergence of "billboard" societies in which every location, institution, activity, event and person becomes a potential carrier of commercial messages.

The erosion of the public sphere by implication undermines diversity of information provision. Cultural diversity becomes the choice markets can offer, but markets tend to offer more of the same, and not fundamentally distinct goods; everything that does not pass the market threshold because there is not a sufficiently large percentage of consumers, disappears. That may be good for markets, it may be suicidal for democratic politics and creative culture.

If public broadcast systems are commercialized, the issue arises whether this leads to a massive inflow of US produced TV materials or to increased opportunities for domestic TV production. It would appear that at least in the short term the creation of free TV markets reinforced the US domination of the images market. There is currently little doubt about the controlling position of US exports on the world TV and film market. This dominance to a large extent follows fairly simple economic mechanisms. The US exporters operate from a very large domestic market that provides the economic resources for a level of investment that facilitates the production of feature films and series that easily have a competitive edge in the world market. Commercialization leads to price wars for the acquisition of successful foreign programmes. This could benefit the foreign sellers, but could also make the domestic alternative an attractive proposition (Waterman. 1988: 147). It could also be that commercial broadcast systems lead to improved revenue bases as channel capacity increases. Initially this could indeed lead to more foreign imports, but with more advertising capacity it could create the resource base for more domestic productions. Waterman argues this option on the basis of the premise that audiences prefer programmes produced within their own country (Waterman. 1988: 144).

The question remains however whether domestic product in fact means localized American, like the French and German issues of Dallas type Hollywood genres. In such cases the language changes, but the genre remains the same.

Deregulation also facilitates the developments of markets for pay-TV type of operations. It is likely that in most pay-TV operations the dominant programme fare will be theatrical films made in the USA. This is so because the USA still maintains a strong competitive advantage in markets for motion pictures and pre-recorded video-cassettes.

In any case it would appear likely that the pressures of privatization will increasingly create commercial incentives for the creation of TV products. This is bound to have an impact on the contents of the products. It will also render the public interest aspirations sought by broadcasters in many countries ever harder to attain. An important policy issue in this connection is whether measures to establish national or regional import quota are effective in stimulating more domestic production. "In order for import quotas governing one media to be effective, alternative delivery systems must also be controlled. A profound blow to this possibility has been forever dealt by the videocassette recorder, a technology whose diffusion and usage is defiant of public control" (Waterman. 1988: 150).

The Trend Towards Globalization

America's hottest export item to-day is pop culture. US movies, music, TV programming and home video now account for some US$8 billion trade surplus. Top sellers are Mickey Mouse, Madonna, Michael Jackson, McDonald's hamburgers, Levi's jeans and Coca-Cola. In the past five years the overseas revenues of Hollywood studios has doubled. The US$20 billion music industry collects some 70% outside the USA. There is world-wide a clear trend towards an increasing demand for the American-brand entertainment. As the *Fortune* magazine recently observed "Around the globe, folks just can't get enough of America".[15] A remarkable feature of this trend is that Europeans and Japanese are buying into this successful export commodity. Of the five global record companies, Warner, CBS, EMI, and Polygram, only Warner is an American corporation. A similar trend is showing in the film industry. The Japanese have invested in the past three years some US$12 billion in the US entertainment companies. In November 1990 Japanese hardware manufacturer Matsushita bought MCA for US$6 billion and acquired with this purchase: Universal Studios, Universal Pictures and MCA Records. Early 1991 Paramount Communications was negotiating with interested Japanese companies (Pioneer and Sumitomo). Also the Disney company has formed a partnership with Japanese investors, among whom Yamaichi Securities and Fuji Bank. By late 1990 an initial US$600 million was provided for film financing.

With these developments the centre of the US film production, Hollywood, has begun to globalize. Feature film production had to take serious account of the growing international demand for entertainment products as a result of the proliferation of commercial TV stations. Joint-ventures have been initiated between Hollywood firms and co-producers from Japan and Russia. Foreign investors have acquired traditional US film "majors", such as Twentieth Century Fox (acquired in 1985 by Rupert Murdoch's News Corporation) and Columbia Pictures (purchased by Japanese Sony in 1989 for US$3.4 billion). The very big media companies have outgrown their saturated home markets and the logical way towards further growth is cross-border expansion. In particular West European and Japanese firms entered the US market loaded with cash from very stable and profitable revenues. A good illustration is the French publishing giant Hachette that in 1988 bought the magazine group Diamandis in the USA. Hachette now owns 74 magazines in 10 countries with total circulation of some 650 copies. Also German Bertelsmann has expanded into the US market with the purchase of publisher Bantam Books, Doubleday and record company RCA Records in 1986. In 1986 German publisher Holtzbrink acquired Holt, Rinehart en and Winston from the publishing branch of CBS.

Recently the European market has seen a great deal of cross-border activity. West-German (Bertelsmann) and French (Hachette) publishers are developing activities in the Spanish market for magazines. Murdoch and Servan-Schreiber have made investments in the Spanish economic press. Robert Hersant, the French tycoon, has acquired provincial newspapers in Spain and Berlusconi, the Italian media baron, has signed contracts for regional TV stations in Spain. Murdoch acquired a 25% interest in the publishers group Grupo Zeta, which is publisher of 4 dailies and 20 magazines. Hachette has acquired interests in the Italian publishing house Rizzoli- Corriere della Sera. The Berlusconi group has had since 1987 investments in West-German cable TV operations (Kabelmediaprogramm Gesellschaft in Munich). The Finivest company (Berlusconi) has a stake in TV station La Cinq. The Maxwell company had a stake in the French TV station TF1.

There are obviously also movements from US companies towards European markets. The US conglomerate Time/Warner collaborates with Hachette and Berlusconi in the *Fortune* editions in France and Italy. Simon & Schuster has bought from Hachette Regents Publishing and the NBC station (owned by General Electric) moved in 1993 into the European TV market through the acquisition of Super Channel.

An important feature of the trend towards globalization is that the trading by the mega-companies is shifting from the international exchange of local products to production for global markets. As the communication conglomerates extend their activities to more countries, the production of culture and information takes on a cosmopolitan hue. The activities of media-barons such as the late Maxwell, Murdoch and Berlusconi in the recently opened Eastern European information markets are telling examples.

Since the changes in East-West relations the countries of Eastern Europe have become important targets for cross-border expansion. In September 1989 Murdoch bought 50% of the shares of the Hungarian daily *Mai Nap* and the weekly *Reform*. It was announced on 3 April 1990 in Budapest that the West-German Springer concern had acquired four regional dailies from the Socialist Party. Together they have 187.000 copies. The company also expressed its intention to invest in the next years some 40 million DM in Hungary, Bulgaria, Poland, and Czecho-Chezcoslovakia. Bertelsmann acquired in July 1990 a majority interest in the daily of the former communist party, the *Nepszabadsag*. The late Maxwell had made investments in the Hungarian press through a 40% interest in the former government paper *Magyar Hirlap*.

Berlusconi has concluded agreements with the Polish TV for the sales of Polish TV programmes on the European market and Hersant (publisher of *Le Figaro* and co-proprietor of French TV station La Cinq) received permission to publish two financial newspapers in the Soviet Union.

Particularly active in Eastern Europe is French advertising giant Havas. In 1990 Havas signed exclusive contracts to sell advertising time on TV networks in East Germany, Czechoslovakia, and Russia. Havas CEO Dauzier also "hopes to plaster billboards all over Eastern Europe".

As this goes on, it is difficult to escape the impression that this globalization is more inspired by cultural conquest than cultural co-existence. When the Hungarian edition of *Playboy* appeared in December 1989, the newspaper advertisement proudly announced that the availability of the magazine represented the freedom the Hungarians had been fighting for. The following month, when McDonald began selling hamburgers in Moscow a company executive announced, "We're going to McDonaldize them" and described this as the company's cultural conquest. Also in early 1990, the French government announced that it was increasing its funding for cultural exports as part of a big cultural campaign to conquer Eastern European countries.

Over the past years the communication industry has become increasingly oriented towards exports and developed ever more interest in collaboration with or acquisition of foreign companies. Some examples of the role of exports are given in Table 11. An interesting case of global expansion is the effort of Playboy Enterprises Inc. to market its videos worldwide through a joint venture with Philips Electronics NV and IBM. Together with these partners interactive CD-ROMs are developed to boost overseas home video sales. In 1992 *Playboy* increased its reach from 17 countries to 64 and the home video division reported an 80% sales increase. As *Playboy* CEO Christie Hefner commented in the *International Herald Tribune* of November 3, 1993: "Starting in 1989, as we saw the clear trend toward privatization of television and satellite delivery overseas plus the growth and penetration of VCR ownership both in the Far East and Europe, we felt that there ought to be some opportunities for *Playboy* to take its programming niche and brand outside of the US".

The growth of exports is among other factors due to rapidly rising costs of production. For example, the major US film companies needed in 1985 a worldwide rental income of US $3.1 billion in order to break even. Their share of foreign earnings has increased between 1983 and 1988 particularly in sales of films for TV distribution from 23% to 57%.

The leading European media companies are presently operational in a number of countries across the world. They are yet to establish a total global presence, but are clearly headed towards this objective (Table 12 gives some examples). Murdoch's News Corporation provides an excellent illustration with its recent invasion of Asia. On July 26, 1993 the owner of Star-TV, Hong Kong billionaire Li Ka-shing, sold 64% of this first Asian satellite TV network to Murdoch for US$525 million.

As *Business Week* projects, "With Star, Murdoch now has a signal that will reach 70% of the world's population by 1995, from Japan to the Middle

East".[16] The deal between Li Ka-shing and Murdoch was largely motivated by the pressure on his network caused by the announcement of Turner (CNN which spends some US$15 million to develop production capacity in Asia), Time-Warner's Home Box Office (on cable in some eight Asian countries), Capital Cities/ABC ESPN (the sports network), the Discovery Channel, and Hong Kong-based Television Broadcasting Inc. to compete with Star TV in 1994 after the launch of a Chinese communications satellite. Other companies entering the huge Asian markets are Dow Jones & Co. and NBC. Both firms are interested in promoting business broadcast news from operations based in Singapore and Hong Kong. Among the driving forces of the globalization processes, the following factors can be observed.

TABLE 11. *Earnings from Exports.*

COMPANY	NATIONALITY	SALES 1989 (IN US$ BILLION)	% OUTSIDE HOME COUNTRY
Philips	Netherlands	30.0	94.0
Reuters	UK	1.9	80.0
Bertelsmann	Germany	6.7	68.0
Sony	Japan	16.3	66.0
IBM	USA	62.7	59.0
NCR	USA	6.0	58.9
Digital	USA	12.7	54.0
Xerox	USA	12.4	54.0
Hewlett-Packard	USA	11.9	53.0
Siemens	Germany	36.3	51.0
Time Warner	USA	10.8	23.0
Disney	USA	4.8	20.0

Technological Development. Technological innovations, especially in the field of informatics, telecommunications and their convergence have largely facilitated processes of globalization. In fact, one could argue that communication/information technologies provide the essential infrastructure for global transactions.

Financial markets. It is likely that the growth of global financial markets in the 1970s triggered off the acceleration of globalization processes. This was reinforced by the rapid proliferation of offshore financial markets and the global circulation of vast amounts of money outside the jurisdiction of national authorities.

TABLE 12. *Companies and Globalization.*

COMPANY	COUNTRIES
Rupert Murdoch	Australia, Great Britain, Germany, France, Spain, the Netherlands, Hungary, USSR, USA, Hong Kong, Fiji, Papua New Guinea.
Bertelsmann	Germany, France, Spain, Belgium, the Netherlands, Great Britain, Sweden, Norway, Denmark, Italy, Switzerland, Austria, Portugal, Greece, USA, Canada, Columbia, Argentina, Brazil, Mexico, Venezuela, Ecuador, Chile, Japan, Australia, New Zealand.
Hachette	France, Monaco, Spain, Italy, Belgium, the Netherlands, Portugal Great Britain, Germany, Sweden, Japan, Hong Kong, China, Brazil, Canada, USA.
Havas	France, Great Britain, Italy, Spain, Belgium, Germany, Czechoslovakia, Soviet Union, Luxembourg, Monaco, USA.
Robert Hersant	France, Belgium, Spain, USA.
Silvio Berlusconi	Italy, Spain, France, Germany.

The Enormous Growth of Trade. Sweeping reductions in costs of air travel and shipping have facilitated phenomenal expansion of cross-border trading. In the process, not only the volume of trade has enormously increased, but also its character has considerably changed. The steeply rising costs of developing new technologies and new products have forced companies to use global brand-names and global advertising within the emerging global markets. The new global approach has meant that corporate strategies focus increasingly on global delivery systems, corporate networks, and electronic markets. Exports and foreign investments in the conventional sense are increasingly replaced by networking arrangements with local delivery systems. Transactions are conducted through transnational data flows that operate through the wide variety of corporate networks that have been created in the past two decades.

Politics. Increasingly in many countries the political climate is very support-ive of globalization processes. The creation of global electronic networks, for example, is largely facilitated through the privatization of public telecom-munication services, the liberalization of electronics markets, and the de-regulation of tariff structures. All such politico-regulatory measures are intended to accommodate the claims of the large corporate users of world communication.

Impact

The impact of globalization will be discussed in terms of fragmentation, McDonaldization, and piracy.

Fragmentation. There are undeniably globalization processes at work to-day. There are trends towards cultural activities spanning the globe. How-ever, despite these realities, there is a strong likelihood that what we are currently witnessing is actually the emergence of a "fragmented globalism" of the world economy (Lanvin. 1991: 99). A remarkable feature of much discourse on globalization completely bypasses the fact that the world is very starkly divided and fractured on many counts. Highly visible fissures are present in the growing economic disparities between both the North and the South and between different social groups within nations.

In the field of world communication, one certainly has to ask "how global is global"? As discussed in chapter two, there remains to-day in the communication field a stark disparity between the affluent industrial nations and the countries of the Third World. If there is a global communi-cations party, the majority of the world's population has not yet been invited to join. As Vijay Menon asks, "But how much a part of the global village is Asia?" (Menon. 1993: 29).

This is obviously an ambiguous situation. Having been left out, has noticeable disadvantages. As the technological infrastructures remain very expensive to acquire and maintain, an important issue will be the possibility that only a limited number of actors will have access to the emerging global circuits. It may well be that the developing countries will experience a "selective short-circuiting" (Lanvin. 1991: 99) of their trading opportunities. However, this may also be a blessing in disguise. It may make those not invited less vulnerable to the problems as posed by the McDonaldization of the world.

Globalization means the emergence of global customers that want global services by global suppliers. These customers (the mega-companies) look for the one-stop agency to provide them with the necessary telecommunication and information network services. They will increasingly push for open access to telecommunication facilities around the world. In accordance with this goal they will lobby strongly for supportive regulatory and technical concepts. So far this has successfully led to the elevation by the ITU of the principle of "interconnectivity"—the norm that compatible networks and services make communication for anyone with anyone possible—to an international legal standard. (Grewlich. 1991: 17). According to the WATTC (the world Administration Telegraph and Telephone) agreement of 1988 interconnectivity provides both for a new legal framework that stimulates innovation in new networks and services, and that protects the developing countries from being cut off the global telecommunications system (Grewlich. 1991: 17).

The question is whether the multilateral fora involved such as GATT, ITU, WIPO, ISO, and UNCTAD will be able to cooperatively address the issue of global open access to networks and services and whether this will be beneficial to only the privileged inhabitants of the "global system" or to all its people. Whatever its blessings may be, for many people the development of a "fragmented globalization" means a continuation of a situation of dependency, exploitation and poverty.

McDonaldization. Today's discourse on globalization suggests the emergence of a global culture. The worldwide proliferation of standardized food, clothing, music, TV drama, Anglosaxon business style and linguistic convention, create the impression of an unprecedented cultural homogenization.

Facilitated by technological innovations, the enormous growth of international trade, and a very supportive liberal political climate, one observes the rapid transnational proliferation of mass-market advertising and electronic entertainment produced by a handful of mega-conglomerates. There is a worldwide spread of commercially packaged cultural products. A uniform consumerist lifestyle is aggressively marketed across the globe.

One could obviously argue that the McDonaldization of the world does not create a uniform, global culture. And one may correctly point to the distinct cultural entities in the world to which the manifold inter-ethnic conflicts are ever so many dramatic testimonies. Or, one could cite the fact that non-Western values are by no means extinct and that an impressive volume of local customs is very much alive around the world.

One could also claim that the project of a global culture is inherently weak as it has no historical and spatial location. A basic ingredient is missing for a global culture. Culture provides people with a sense of identity, a past, destiny, and dignity. Culture is bound to time and space. McDonaldization is a-historical and spatially non-located. It is hard to see that people can identify with it or derive dignity from it.

But even if "global culture" is not an adequate category of analysis, there is undoubtedly a process of "cultural globalization". A lively expression of cultural globalization are the Disney amusement parks, whether in Tokyo Disneyland or Paris Disneyland that opened in the spring of 1992. "We're going to be American because America sells really well", says Robert Fitzpatrick, president of Euro Disneyland, the 5,000-acre park just East of Paris. The French who occasionally have been in strong opposition against USA cultural imperialism have received "this shrine of American pop culture" enthusiastically despite some critics describing the Disney invasion as a "cultural Chernobyl" (Marguerite Duras). As a matter of fact the French government has reduced the value added tax on theme parks from 18.6 % to 7%, lent 4 billion francs at preferential rates and provided 2.7 billion francs in infrastructure improvements, such as highways and rail roads. [17] Ironically, it turns out in late 1993 that Euro Disney is not very successful and has already lost over US$1 billion. Among the arguments for the limited interest that French people show for the American project, is that no wine drinking is allowed in the amusement park.

The McDonald type cultural conquest has an important impact on economic development patterns and may well raise serious obstacles for self-reliant economies. Its greatest success is the world-wide emergence of consumer societies. McDonaldization sells very persuasively a consumerist, resource-intensive lifestyle that this world's ecology can ill afford. What matters most is that McDonaldization reduces local cultural space. The process of cultural globalization is engineered by forces that are intent on reducing local cultural space. The aggressive around-the-clock marketing, the controlled information flows that do not confront people with the long-term effects of an ecologically detrimental lifestyle, the competitive advantage against local cultural providers, the obstruction of local initiative, all converge into a reduction of local cultural space.

The process of globalization has given rise to a concern about the nationality of media-ownership. Ironically, in the USA, there has been an expression of serious worry about the Japanese take-over of traditional Hollywood companies. However, this concern tends to lead attention away from the more basic problem: globalization increases the mega-corporate control over the provision of information and culture. As Schiller writes, "The daily instruction of most Americans is now in the hands not of the schools but of the corporate multimedia packagers" (Schiller. 1990: 829). There would seem a very realistic chance that the "Lords of the Global Village" (Bagdikian. 1989) will control before the turn of the century most of the world's expression, creativity, and instruction. With the globalization of informational and cultural production, it will no longer be just the US transnational companies, but also the Dutch, German, and Japanese firms which will use information and culture to sell consumerism across the globe. Maintaining American style and production values, media products have now become "the generic material for all transnationals, whatever their ownership base".

Fusing different sources of capital, the global transnational information and cultural producers are "turning the world into a shopping mall for those with sufficient disposable income" (Schiller. 1993: 29 and 40).

There are also instances where the global operators have understood that adaptations to local taste make their exploits even more successful. The performance of the music television station, MTV, on the Asian markets is a good case in point. MTV beams its signals to Asian audiences through one of the channels on Satellite Television Asian Region (STAR TV). This Hong Kong based satellite operator reaches out to some 3.75 million households in Asian countries. With many Asian youngsters ready to spend on global tastes this is clearly a promising market for MTV advertisers. In order to accommodate local taste, some 20% of MTV programming is Asian. This includes the promotion of Thai and Chinese pop stars and Mandarin sung Mando-Rock music.

MTV products may be regionally customized, its prime orientation remains to offer advertisers a profitable market for consumer products and to lure consumers, particularly young ones, to watch its programmes and in the process influence their tastes, life styles, and moral values. This cultural adaptation is also a concern of those TV companies that are trying to cash in on the expansion of pay-TV markets in Latin America. Among the contenders are Turner Broadcasting, ESPN, NBC (with 24 hour Spanish-language news), MTV Latino, and Murdoch's Fox Latin America channel. Although pay-TV only reaches a limited portion of Latin American TV households, it represents an affluent and a growing market for advertisers. In order to make the programming more acceptable to local audiences, they are given Latin looks. As the vice-president of Fox Latin America comments, "you have to add the salsa to it".[18]

Opinions differ regarding the effect of cultural globalization. For the Asian region one finds those defending an optimist position, "We in Asia have a particular advantage . . . nobody has yet moulded us. . . . even in the most economically advanced Asian societies, we are a very tradition-minded people" (Joseph Wang, advertising expert from Hong Kong quoted by Menon. 1993: 31) against anthropologist Santasombat from Thailand (Yos Santasombat, quoted by Menon. 1993: 31) "Thai society today is indeed in a state of confusion and expedient westernisation. McDonalds, Burger King, Dunkin Donuts. Fast foods and fast profits—Thai culture and traditions are becoming obsolete and irrelevant, if not outright obstacles to modernisation and westernisation".

The concern about the cultural and economic impact of globalization is not restricted to Third World countries. The expansion of the US cultural industries has become a hot political issue in Europe. In September 1993 the French audiovisual industry has taken the initiative to protest against the inclusion of audiovisual products in the final text of the Uruguay Round GATT negotiations. In these negotiations, the USA demanded that the world trade in audiovisual products follows the principles of a free trade regime. This implies that a variety of protectionist measures (such as national import quota and state subsidies) which are common in European countries are abandoned.

In a countermove representatives of the French entertainment sector (with the support of the EC Ministers of Culture) have claimed that only removing audiovisual products from GATT rules can save the European film and entertainment industry. An appeal signed by over 4,000 professionals in the industry accuses the USA of 'cultural dumping'. Important considerations for the French action were the 22 billion francs European trade deficit with the USA in audiovisual trade and the fact that some 80% of movies exhibited in European cinemas are made in the USA against only 2% European films released in the USA. The European film industry is convinced that subjecting its sector to free trade implies a global spread of Hollywood materials and the effective annihilating of European culture.

Piracy. There has always been an economic interest in intellectual property. This interest developed into real trade concerns only in the 1970s and 80s. Increasingly the economic significance of trade in intellectual property provides the rationale for protective policy measures. Globalization does raise risks for intellectual property rights holders. "American pop culture has become so popular that lots of folks out there are stealing it."[19] The Motion Pictures Association of America estimates a US$1.2 billion annual loss to film and video piracy. Bangkok is the classical case: increasingly characterized by globalized market taste. The Central Mall on Saturday afternoon means young Thais crowding in such places as Pizza Hut or Kentucky Fried Chicken and visiting cinemas for Robocop 2. The MPAA calls Bangkok "the worst offender in the Far East". Well-organized, very lucrative piracy operations in video and audio cater to these global tastes. In Thailand alone the music and film industry claims to loose annually some US$70 million to pirates.[20] Annually over 150 million illegal cassettes are distributed through some 12,000 videoparlors. Since 1987 the US government has cancelled trade privileges for Thailand upon the strong lobbying of the International Intellectual Property Alliance (IIPA).

The Motion Picture Association is reported to have spent some US$20 million in 1990 for its global struggle against piracy of entertainment. In 59 countries almost 6,000 raids were conducted. The major forms of piracy are: unauthorized public exhibition, theft of film prints, distribution of illegal video cassettes, and theft of broadcast signals. According to *Business Week* (February 10, 1992) piracy represents a loss of sales around the world of some US$17 billion annually (see Table 13). Piracy is considered by US industries a crucial trade barrier. Intellectual property theft is seen as an obstacle to worldwide market access. The industry argues that safer intellectual property rights environments will increase their export and local production. This is important since in many profitable industrial areas the real growth is abroad. The movie industry is strongly interested in strict copyright protection in foreign countries to expand its markets (see Table 14). A classical example is South Korea. When the South Korean government began to act against local pirates the result was an increase of US film industries revenues from South Korea from US$ 7 million in 1988 to some US$100 million in 1991.[21]

Stricter rules on intellectual property protection obviously affect those who make a good living out of piracy. But it goes much further. The sort of intellectual property protection that Western states and their transnational corporations want to impose worldwide has a fundamentally negative impact on the possibilities for Third World countries to develop local technologies and cultural expressions.

Summary

In today's world communication four major trends can be observed. Digitization, consolidation, deregulation, and globalization affect people's lives around the globe in important ways. In the last chapter we shall analyse how the accumulated effects of these current trends disempower people and how people can begin to resist this.

Notes

1. Source Inter Press Service. January 4. 1992.
2. Source *Business Week*. *October* 7. 1991.
3. *Business Week*. October 7. 1991.
4. Forester. 1990: 467.
5. *Business Week*. January 20. 1992: 34-39.
6. *Business Week*. October 14. 1991: 40.
7. *Business Week*. October 14. 1991: 41.
8. *Business Week*. October 7. 1991: 60
9. *Business Week*. October 25. 1993: 34.
10. *Fortune*. December 1990.
11. Source for fiscal year ended June 30, 1990: *Business Week*. November 5. 1990: 27.
12. The irony of the Matsushita purchase of MCA is that the Music Corporation of America tried in the 1970s through a US Supreme Court action to block the sales of the home video recorder and to-day is owned by one the world's largest manufacturers of VCRs. In *Fortune*. December 31. 1990: 30.
13. *Business Week*. December 19. 1990. Fiscal year ended March 31, 1990.
14. Source First Boston Corp. Quoted in *Business Week*. September, 17. 1990: 53.
15. *Fortune*. December 31. 1990: 28.
16. *Business Week*. August 9.1993: 21.

17. *International Herald Tribune*. April 9. 1992: 1.
18. *Fortune*. December 31. 1990: 34.
19. *Business Week*. November 1, 1993: 28.
20. IPS report of December 7, 1990.
21. *Business Week*. September 21. 1991.

References

Bagdikian, B.H. (1989). "The Lords of the Global Village". In *The Nation*. June 12. 805-820.

Forester, T. & Morrison, P. (1990) "Computer Unreliability and Social Vulnerability". In *Futures*. Vol. 22. No. 5. 462-474.

Fuhr, J.P. (1990). "Telephone subsidization of rural areas in the USA". In *Telecommunications Policy*. Vol. 14. No. 3. 183-188.

Gershon, R.A. (1990). "Global cooperation in an era of deregulation". In *Telecommunications Policy*. Vol. 14. No. 3. 249-259.

Graaf, F. de. (*et al.*) (1990). *"Juridische aspekten van netwerken"*. Utrecht: Netherlands Association for Computers and Law.

Grewlich, K.W. (1990). "Cooperative Communication Policies". In *Transnational Data and Communication Report*. Vol. 13. No. 2. 10-12

Hills, J. (1989). Universal Service. "Liberalization and privatization of telecommunications". In *Telecommunications Policy*. Vol. 13. No. 2. 129-144.

Lanvin, B. (1991). "Information, strategies and infrastructures for international trade". In *Communications & Strategies*. No. 1. 97-102.

Lee, M.A. (1991). "Arms and the media: business as usual". In *Index on Censorship*. 10. 29-31.

McQuail,D. (1992). *Media Performance*. London: Sage.

Menon, V. (1993). "Tradition meets modernity on the path to the global village". In *Intermedia*. Vol. 21. No 1. 29-31.

OECD .(1990). "Performance Indicators for Public Telecommunications Operators." *Information Computer Communications Policy*. No. 22.

Redeker, H. (1989). "Liability in Telecommunication Systems; The German Case." In *International Computer Law Adviser*. Vol. 4. No. 1. 18-21.

Robinson, D. Campbell, Buck, E.B. & Cuthbert, M. (1991). "Music at the Margins. " *Popular Music and Global Cultural Diversity*. London: Sage.

Russo, J., Hale, T.C. & Helm, R. S. (1989). "Computer Viruses: New Potential Liability for Software Developers and Expert System Providers." In *International Computer Law Adviser*. 4-13.

Saxby, S. (1990). "The Role of Law in the Development of the Information Society." In *Kasperen*, H.W.K. & Oskamp, A. [Eds.]. Amongst Friends in Computers and Law. Deventer: Kluwer. 213-228.

Schiller, D. & Fregoso, R.L. (1991). "A private view of the digital world." In *Telecommunications Policy*. Vol. 15. No. 3. 195-208.

Schiller, H.I. (1990). *The Nation*, December 31.

Schiller, H.I. (1993). *Mass Communications and American Empire*. Revised edition. Boulder: Westview.

Sieber, U. (1986). *The International Handbook on Computer Crime*. New York: John Wiley & Sons.

Stuurman, K. (1990). "Legal Aspects of Standardization and Certification of Information Technology and Telecommunication: An Overview." In Kasperen, H.W.K. & Oskamp, A. (Eds.). *Amongst Friends in Computers and Law*. Deventer: Kluwer. 75-92.

Vandenberghe, G.V.P. (1988). "Software Bugs: A Matter of Life and Liability". In *International Computer Law Adviser*. 18-22.

Vries, H. de. (1990). Home-telematics and Privacy Protection. In Kasperen, H.W.K. & Oskamp, A. (Eds.). *Amongst Friends in Computers and Law*. Deventer: Kluwer. 201-212.

Waterman, D. (1988). "The Economic Effects of Privatization and New Technology". In *Telecommunications Policy*. Vol. 12. No. 2. 141-151.

CHAPTER FOUR

World Communication and Self-Empowerment

"The people are the most important element in a country; the spirits of the land and the grain are secondary; and the sovereign is the least"

Mencius (371-289 BC; disciple of Confucius).

This last chapter argues that the current trends in world communication converge towards the disempowerment of people. They contribute to the establishment of a new world order which is inegalitarian, exclusive, and elite-oriented. Against this process emerges the aspiration of citizenship in a world community which is egalitarian, inclusive, and people-centred. In this community people are the most important element. The realization of this aspiration will largely depend upon the determination of people to empower themselves.

World Communication and Local Space

The images of CNN do not exactly transform our world into a village. In the first chapter this fashionable image was criticized as a very inadequate description of the real world. However, although for most people life takes place in limited time and space, it has become increasingly difficult to separate the local from the global. To-days' world politics is characterized by the interconnectedness of the global and the local. This global/local intersection means that decision making on the global level does affect local situations, often in dramatic ways. For example, World Bank global plans that originate in Washington have a far-reaching effect on local rain forest communities and their chances of survival. The Tropical Forestry Action Plan initiated by the World Bank, the United Nations Development Programme and the US Agency for International Development in 1985 was a US$8 billion plan to save tropical forests. This plan, according to the critical analysis made by the World Rainforest Movement, if implemented, would increase the harm inflicted upon the forest dwellers. Another evident case of the global/local interconnection is the direct, local impact on people's lives of the structural adjustment policies demanded by the International Monetary Fund. Whenever global policies impose the cutting of expenditures in essential public services, such as for example in Peru in August 1990, the immediate result is a staggering increase of absolute poverty among people in local communities.

More examples could be given, such as the employment policies enacted globally by transnational corporations and their local effect on the working force, or the activities of global human rights organizations and their impact on local victims of human rights violations and their tormentors. An important implication of global/local relations is that local struggle is not sufficient. If, for example, local communities want to retain an autonomous cultural space, their battleground has to go beyond the local boundaries, since the space for local cultural expression is co-determined by such global policies, as GATT decisions on trade in services or on intellectual property rights.

The global/local intersection also implies that the local situation can have global reach and world politics may find its origin in local issues. Local conflicts, such as the Iran-Iraq war, or the Iraq-Kuwait conflict, have decisive repercussions on the world level. It should also be observed that the foreign policy conduct of many governments is dictated by its domestic roots. The domestic politics of powerful lobbies will strongly influence a country's position in world political fora. A case in point are the effective lobbies of industrialists and farmers in Northern countries and their impact in the GATT multilateral trade negotiations.

Like world politics, world communication also affects the local space in which people around the globe lead their daily lives. This happens primarily when people are consumers of the products of world communication. For those who have direct access to the mass media the confrontation with the words, sounds and images of global TV operators, world news agencies, mega advertisers, or transnational music producers, is hard to avoid. Much of their audiovisual entertainment, advertising fare, and musical experiences will be provided by a handful of cultural moguls. On this level of impact, people may also be users of services the world communication industry offers. The quality, reliability, and affordability of such services as international mail and telephony are important factors in the lives of many people.

On a different level of impact, people's lives are important as objects of world communication. This means that people constitute the raw material for world news reporting, for TV documentaries or for book publishing. As such, world attention may be focused on their drama (if they are Bosnian refugees, for example), on the problems they cause for foreign tourists (if they are Brazilian street children), on the risks they pose (if they are young Thai prostitutes), or on what we can do for them (if they are political prisoners adopted by Amnesty International). Without world communication only few people would know about fellow human beings in the rain forests of Sarawak or in the devastating civil war of Angola. People as objects of world communication can also imply that people's stories or songs are used and formatted for sales on a global market.

World communication affects in indirect ways also those people who lack electricity, are illiterate, or live in remote communities. Their lives are often influenced by decisions and choices made by others who are world communication consumers. In many Third World countries the adoption of the lifestyles propagated by global advertising in the urban centres, has a deleterious economic effect on the rural population.

World Communication and Disempowerment

In order to defend the position that current trends in world communication and their different forms of impact contribute to the disempowerment of people, it should be clarified what disempowerment means. The term "disempowerment" literally means making people powerless. It refers to a process in which people loose the capacity to control decisions affecting their lives. Disempowerment is the reduction of people's ability to define themselves and to construct their own identities.

Disempowerment can be both the outcome of a deliberate strategy (the process is intentional) or the unintended outcome of human acting (the process is coincidental). In the case of the latter process, disempowerment can be the result of a series of mutually reinforcing factors that in themselves do not intend to incapacitate people. It may even be that acts aimed at enabling people have an unintended opposite outcome. We know from our own experience that intentions and outcomes of human acting can be very different. Well-intended efforts at increasing people's abilities can have the unintended effect of increasing their dependence. The classical example comes from African countries where women walk long distances to the common well to get water. Concerned development experts designed tap water facilities in the homes of these women thus expecting to increase their independence. Since the water well was the unique forum for collective exchange of information and experience, it formed a basis for women's empowerment. The isolation in individual kitchens undermined the development of solidarity. A very different example comes from the intention to protect people's privacy against the collection of electronic data. The privacy laws through which legislators want to give people a level of control over data collections, tend to domesticate the privacy issue. This means that although a limited form of enabling people takes place, the very fact of collecting data about people remains as it was. The long term effect of this will be a basic erosion of people's capacity to resist the use of person-linked data in cases where less than benign states decide to use data against their citizens.

A very real possibility is also that the acting subject (for example an individual newsreporter) tries to perform a professional job with the aim to provide information that facilitates people's independent decision making. However, the overall industrial organisation in which he or she functions, may format the information in ways that increase people's ignorance.

Very often disempowerment occurs through active intervention by some social actors who intentionally reduce the capacity of other social actors for self-governance. A dramatic illustration of intentional disempowerment was the South African policy of apartheid. This was a deliberate strategy to keep the majority of a country's people dependent and ignorant. Disempowerment as strategy often employs the deceit of making people believe that existing conditions are desirable and preferred out of free will. The most perverse form of disempowerment makes people accept their own dependency and second rate position. Intentional disempowerment serves hegemonic purposes and is employed in a variety of social situations where some actors stand to benefit from the submissiveness of other actors. These situations range from marital relations to the world economy. A complicating factor in the intentional process is the real possibility of people inviting their own disempowerment. Illustrative of this are doctor-patient relations in which people actively invite the medical expert to take control over their lives.

Disempowerment as strategy tends to be employed by those in positions of power as a self-evident necessity and tends to be accepted as inevitable by those targeted for submission. Disempowerment can even be invited by the less powerful themselves and it can also be the coincidental result of non hegemonic acts. The question this raises is whether disempowerment should be a cause for concern?

The answer will obviously depend upon the normative framework one selects for the judgment of the quality of human life. If this framework is defined by the respect and defence of basic human rights (as embodied in the standards of international human rights law), disempowerment causes serious concern because it violates fundamental human entitlements to respect for everyone's dignity, equality, and liberty. Human rights represent the protection of people's right to express themselves, to freely associate, and to organize themselves. Human rights guarantee people active participation in political life, in science, technology and culture, access to knowledge, and the kind of information provision that enables them to make independent decisions. All this is undermined by disempowerment which violates at the core the basic human right to individual autonomy and integrity.

Since it is possible that disempowerment is invited by the disempowered, the question comes up whether a concern about this voluntary act is an expression of paternalism? There are obviously various options in this situation. People in developing countries, for example, may want to enjoy the attractions of capitalist modernity and indulge in the good life of Marlboro. Criticism of this preference contains the danger of sliding towards the paternalist position of the critique of "false consciousness", or, worse, of a romanticised "anti-modernism" (Tomlinson. 1991:108-121). What precisely is in the interest of an agent, is difficult, if not impossible to define from the outside. It would be hard to defend, for example, that one can know the true interests of those who invite exogenous cultural standards.

It may well be however that people are genuinely unaware that embracing the gospel of global advertising entails the dependency of the compulsive consumer. In this case there would seem nothing wrong with sounding some warning bells. This is no more paternalist than the scientist who warns people of the dangers of nuclear waste. It is after the warning that people themselves should decide what to do. One should also be aware of the real possibility that the choice for forms of dependency is only in a limited sense a free choice. Such choices are rarely made by the people themselves, but rather by their governing elites. Secondly, the realities of the world system often coerce people into making these choices. The recent GATT negotiations have provided many illustrations of how conditions of dependence are accepted as a result of multilateral or bilateral pressures. Countries have been coerced (usually through bi-lateral negotiations with the USA or the European Union) in changing their position through threats of sanctions from Western trading partners. The real policy decisions have not been taken in the GATT forum, but in these bi-lateral encounters. A classical case provides Mexico where president Carlos Salinas de Gortari who wanted a North American Free Trade Agreement (NAFTA) was put under enormous pressure by US copyright industries that threatened not to support the agreement if Mexico would not toughen its intellectual property protection. US trade pressures also forced Mexico to enact a Law for the Promotion and Protection of Industrial Property (effective June 28, 1991) that provides for patent protection for plant varieties. Mexico was rewarded for its accommodation of US interests by removal from the US blacklist of trading partners (the Special 301 list).

One may firmly believe that even if people make the wrong choice, it is best that they make their own choices. Yet, this does not mean that these choices could not be criticized, rejected, or called to account for. Also forms of disempowerment actively supported by the disempowered can be measured against the norm of respect for human dignity, autonomy and integrity.

In disempowerment strategies communication is often recognized by those intent on reducing people's power as an effective tool. World communication furthers people's disempowerment since the major technological trend (digitization) creates new forms of dependency and vulnerability, the trends towards consolidation and deregulation reinforce censored access to information and limit use of knowledge resources, the trend towards globalization creates a cultural environment that victimizes people, spreads compulsive consumerism and reduces local cultural space. To support this position the following illustrations are selected.

Digital Technologies

The proliferation of digital technologies disempowers people through new forms of dependence and vulnerability. Intrusive modes of electronic surveillance make people's lives transparent. Living in glass houses makes people vulnerable to Big Brother-type of external decision making that is difficult to control. Not knowing who has what sort of information on you creates a state of dependency. Modern states spend considerable energy spying on their own citizens, gathering and storing massive amounts of information through which they keep their citizens under "around-the-clock" surveillance in good Orwellian fashion. The ensuing loss of control is compounded by an increasing dependence upon digital technologies that are pervasive, ill-understood (even by the experts and technocrats) and that have a potentially very damaging impact. The rapidly increasing scope of information provision around the world thanks to digital technologies, also confronts more and more people with a dependence upon data that may be incomplete by intent or default. These developments make people increasingly powerless. They seriously reduce the capacity of ordinary men and women to control decisions that others take about their lives. These decisions may be based on information that is incorrect, that should have been private or voluntarily and conciously sharedwith others. Moreover, if people have to rely upon technologies they do not understand, they also have to rely upon experts who claim to understand these technologies. In fact they delegate control over their lives to the technocrats. This dependence is corroborated by the abscence of robust remedial measures in case the technologies or the experts fail.

Access to Knowledge

Restraining people's access to knowledge is a common tool of disempowerment strategies. Dominance does not only operate through imposition, but also through deprivation. Many of the good things that have been developed in the West, for example, are not shared with the Third World. Most of what the West transfers to the Third World is among the lowest of what it produces. This is not accidental. Take the case of Western technology which is jealously protected from transfer as it is considered private property of the "knowledge-producers".

Related to this is the privatization and commercialization of the production of knowledge. As a result of the trends towards deregulation and globalization, the market place has become the leading actor in determining the direction and scope of knowledge production. As knowledge is created and controlled as private property, knowledge as common good is destroyed. This is the inherent meaning of privatization (private =to deprive), it deprives communities of access to their common heritage and renders this the entitlement of individual owners.

The emerging international intellectual property rights regime transforms common heritage into exclusive, private (corporate) property. A case in point are the world's biological systems which are common heritage, but which through technological innovations (biotechnology) are now becoming private property.

Against the rather successful movement of Western states and Transnational Corporations to incorporate the protection of intellectual property rights in a GATT agreement, a large meeting of NGOs maintained that such an agreement would seriously hinder the diffusion of technical knowledge to Third World countries, hamper local technological innovation and benefit mainly Transnational Corporations. "The free flow of scientific knowledge and information within the scientific community would be severely restricted. It would therefore obstruct the very development of science and technology in the public interest . . . the proposals aim at reserving the domestic markets of the Third World countries for the manufactured goods of the developed countries. The proposals would arrest the promotion of indigenous technological capabilities" (New Delhi Statement on Intellectual Property Rights & Obligations, March 1990).

The global harmonization of protection of intellectual property rights (IPR) that is proposed by the GATT agreement, is supported with the argument that this will increase technology transfer to Third World countries and will facilitate access to advanced technology. Given their export orientation many developing countries have accepted to change their IPR domestic regulation to a level defined by the industrialized countries. By now many of them have adopted the GATT provisions on Trade Related Intellectual Property Rights (TRIPS) which determines global minimal norms for protection. Several countries have already revised their IPR laws.

There is a clear shift from the earlier position taken by the Third World countries. Most of them now feel that only adopting the proposed harmonization can reduce the North-South technology gap. In connection with the technology gap many countries have begun to focus on export strategies and the common expectation is that improved IPR protection will reinforce this economic policy through transfer of technology and cooperation in science and technology. It is still far from clear whether the shift in position will indeed benefit the Third World. In any case given the great differentiation among Third World countries, the effects are likely to be different across countries. It may well be that only very few countries will benefit through the new IPR regime and have more technology imports, more domestic innovation, and more R & D investment. The likelihood is, however, that the majority of countries will not see any such benefits and may even confront strong drawbacks. It is likely, for example, that prices for the products of biotechnological engineering will increase.

It would have been unrealistic to expect otherwise, as the global imposition of the new IPR regime is not motivated by a strong desire to share the world's knowledge and to reduce ignorance, but by the need to control expanding markets. The emerging regime for the global control of knowledge demonstrates the effective employment of the strategy of disempowerment for the benefit of the transnational corporate interests.

The GATT TRIPS agreement sanctions that the biotechnology industry commercializes and privatises the biodiversity of the Third World countries. This industry uses the genetic resources of the Third World as a free common resource and then transforms them in laboratories in patentable genetically engineered products. In the process the industry manipulates life-forms that are common heritage. This means that whereas formerly plants and animals were excluded from the IPR regime, biotechnology has changed this. Life can now be the object of ownership. This has many perplexing implications, one of which is that thousands of years of local knowledge about life organisms are devalued and replaced by the alleged superior knowledge of Western scientists and engineers.

Cultural Production

In the field of cultural production, disempowerment operates through the creation of a cultural environment in which victimization, compulsive consumerism, loss of local cultural space reinforce dependency. Modern markets tend to keep their clients under control by inundating them with avalanches of non-stop distractions which suggest, as Aldous Huxley phrased it in *Brave New World* "everybody is happy now". In these distractions sex and violence figure prominently.

Violence tends to be presented in ways which make people fearful of becoming victims and thus paralyse them. "Constant displays of violent power and victimization cultivate an exaggerated sense of danger and insecurity among heavy viewers of television. That is the most pervasive and debilitating consequence of daily exposure to television violence. What we call the 'mean world syndrome' contributes to a loss of sensitivity and trust, demonstrates power for some and vulnerability for others, and invites violence and victimization" (Gerbner. 1992: 1). A massive choreography of violence has become an essential component of the cultural environment in which people live and children are born. This disempowers people since it creates deep feelings of dependence particularly in those most likely to be portrayed as the victims: women and minorities. TV violence facilitates disempowerment as the resulting insecurity tends to lead to requests for the mechanisms whereby the power holders control their environment: more prisons, more police, more repression.

Global entertainment also employs on a grand scale gendered stereotypes that misrepresent and disempower women. These images portray women as second class citizens, sexually available, and dependent.

A special case of disempowerment operates through the reduction of local cultural space. Whether a community will be able to develop its own cultural identity (to empower itself culturally) will largely depend upon the local cultural space people can control. If people are to be "beings for themselves" (Freire. 1972: 129), they need sufficient cultural space to define their identity autonomously. If this space is not adequately provided or acquired, they will be incorporated in structures of oppression that define people as "beings for others".

Local cultural space is a battleground. There are always hegemonic forces inside and outside the community intent on reducing this space and thus diminishing people's capacity for autonomous choice. To-day the local cultural space of many communities across the world is threatened by the process of cultural globalization. Facilitated by technological innovations, the enormous growth of international trade, and a very supportive liberal political climate, one observes the rapid transnational proliferation of mass-market advertising and electronic entertainment produced by a handful of mega-conglomerates. There is a worldwide spread of commercially pack-aged cultural products. A uniform consumerist lifestyle is aggressively marketed across the globe. This process is engineered by forces intent on the reduction of local cultural space. This obstructs the local initiative and disadvantages the local cultural producers. It effectively silences local culture and hampers people's development as "beings for themselves". The Latin American author Eduardo Galeano once observed in an interview that the Latin American identity is largely defined by those neo-liberal policies that the North passionately promotes, and exports, but seldom applies to itself. These policies stimulate consumption and kill creativity. They de-velop in Latin Americans, according to Galeano, a trend towards imitation and a "mentality of resignation". Galeano's analysis is also valid outside Latin America. The mentality of resignation is a widespread phenomenon and signals that disempowerment has been successful.

The global spread of capitalist modernity and its agents such as adver-tising, do not merely introduce specific products on local markets, but promote a culture that overshadows local knowledge and experience and that creates dependence and hampers autonomous development.

Empowerment

If we are concerned about disempowerment of people—whether intention-ally or coincidentally—it is crucial to design modes of resistance. The obvious response to disempowerment would seem to be empowerment. Empowerment as response to intentional disempowerment would be confrontational as it aims to resist hegemonic forces. Empowerment as response to coincidental disempowerment would be cooperative since all actors involved share similar intentions.

The term empowerment literally means that people are given power. It refers to a process in which people achieve the capacity to control decisions affecting their lives. Empowerment enables people to define themselves and to construct their own identities. Empowerment can be the outcome of an intentional strategy which is either initiated externally by empowering agents or solicited by disempowered people. Empowerment can also be coincidental in which case it happens as a result of human acts that did not intent to capacitate people or that even intended to disempower people.

Much like communication is an important tool of disempowerment, it plays a significant role in empowerment. People's power requires knowledge about the decisions that affect their lives and information about what they can do about these decisions. People's power also needs expression, dialogue and the sharing of experiences. There is a variety of approaches to empowerment of people in the context of world communication. As illustrations in the following approaches are selected.

The Regulatory Approach. Using the regulatory approach to empowerment means that legislation, jurisprudence, and self-regulation provide possibilities for people to seek redress against undue invasion of their privacy, to achieve access to information held by governments, to exercise the right of reply or to represent minority viewpoints or minority languages in the mainstream mass media.

An example of the regulatory approach to empowerment is provided by the case law in connection with Article 10 of the European Convention on Human Rights and Fundamental Freedoms. The essential part of this article reads "Everyone has the right to freedom of expression. This right shall include freedom to hold opinions and to receive and impart information and ideas without interference by public authority and regardless of frontiers". In the opinion of the European Court of Human Rights this article constructs a right to receive information and ideas, not just broadcast signals and it imposes upon broadcasters the duty to accommodate this receivers' right. According to the jurisprudence of the European Court the European citizen has the right to be properly informed. In several opinions the Court has stated that not only do the mass media have a right to impart information, they have the task "to impart information and ideas on matters of public interest", and the public has a right to receive such information and ideas. The European Court has ruled that the media are purveyors of information and public watchdogs. This matches with a classical opinion of the US Supreme Court in the Red Lion Broadcasting versus the FCC in 1969: "the right of the viewers and listeners, not the right of broadcasters is paramount."

Another example are the various rules on a right of reply in different legislations. These rules vary from the entitlement to respond to critical opinions to a right of reply to factual allegations. In countries that recognize this provision the reply is usually published in the offending newspaper. If newspapers refuse this, the persons who feel wronged may in some countries (for example in France and Spain) seek redress through the assistance of a court of law.

Also forms of voluntary professional self-regulation may aim at people's empowerment in relation to the institutions of mass communication. Examples are national press councils (for example in Australia, Austria, the Netherlands, Norway, Sweden, and the UK) which hear complaints from individuals about the performance of the press. Some countries have in addition to the press council a Press Ombudsman (Sweden) who may arbitrate in conflicts between the public and the press, in other countries the newspapers themselves have their own ombudsman (for example in Canada). Guidance for decisions about complaints is often provided by the standards articulated in professional codes of conduct. A common outcome of the council's proceedings is the obligation for papers to publish the council's decisions. The regulatory approach has several weaknesses. Access to the law courts is often complex, time consuming and costly, and the outcome is insecure. In the case of self regulation the effectiveness is dependent upon the compliance by the offenders. It remains a voluntary arrangement with no formal obligations towards the complainants. In many countries there are no adequate legal provisions that enable people to resist forms of disempowerment through public communication. Only few countries have strong constitutional provisions on the protection of privacy. A formal right of reply is not recognized in most countries.

Access legislation is still an underdeveloped field around the world. In many countries the legal provisions on freedom of speech are insufficient to protect people against political and/or commercial censorship of the mass media. Actually, in many countries constitutional guarantees of freedom of speech do not exclude that many people (for example military officers, civil servants, editors of school and university newspapers, or children in the family) are silenced much of the time.

The flaw of the regulatory approach is also the assumption of equality before the law. In the reality of law enforcement the interests of the powerful are better served in spite of formal equality. They know better how to use the law and they are often the "repeat players" who normally win against the "one shotters". "Whilst one-shotters tend to be individuals with relatively limited resources, repeat players tend to be organizations which are financially far better equipped to initiate or undertake legal action. This gives repeat players considerable advantages and so further emphasizes problems of inequality in obtaining access to the legal system, and, more importantly, of being able successfully to mobilize this system to their own advantage" (Tomasic. 1985: 53).

In conventional law enforcement, equality before the law means the Lockean standard of "one rule for rich and poor". In this interpretation the law recognizes a formal concept of equality that is related to the perception of inequality as a form of social differentiation which can and should be corrected. Law is anti-discriminatory in the sense of repairing social disadvantage by the equal treatment of unequals. This however does not change the structurally unequal relations of power. The equal treatment can even reinforce the inequality. Providing equal liberties to unequal parties functions in the interest of the most powerful.

The Educational Approach. This approach addresses the need to make people critically aware of how media are organized, how they function, and how their contents can be analysed. Media education takes place in many countries in different formats including public awareness campaigns, formal school programmes (in primary, secondary and tertiary education), and informal workshops with a range of social groups, such as religious organizations or youth clubs. An example of informal media education comes from South Africa where the Community Arts Protect (CAP) ran in 1993 a first workshop for women on video and TV. The rationale for the exercise was the conviction that "The status of women in society cannot be addressed by simply offering them production skills. The political analysis of media must be included so that women can then change and challenge its content" (Du Toit. 1993: 8). As part of the workshop some twenty women viewed TV advertisements "exploring the way in which mainstream media television excluded certain audience groups in terms of both race and gender" (Du Toit. 1993: 8). The workshop offered also practical skills training in video.

Media education is based upon the observation that both children and adults spend large amounts of their time as media audiences and that this makes it necessary to develop a critical appreciation of the media product or, as it is also called, a media literacy. In some countries, media education has developed fairly extensively (for example, Australia, Brazil, Canada, France, Germany, India, Japan, the Netherlands, New Zealand, the UK, the USA, and the Nordic countries) whereas in other countries (for example most African countries and the Arab states) it has hardly begun.

In several countries, women's groups have actively engaged in media education. They have initiated discussions on the representation of women in the media and have managed in some countries (for example Australia) to have pornographic images in films or advertisement withdrawn. Although several European countries have officially expressed the need for media education, rarely does one find clear articulations of what this includes. In Finland the objectives of media education have been formulated as: to train pupils to observe and interpret media messages, to guide pupils in the selective and critical reception of media messages, to encourage pupils to form independent opinions based on media information as well as other sources of communication.

The education approach has various problems. Even in countries with a strong tradition in this field, media education tends to be provided on an *ad hoc* basis (Germany), or largely as an extra-curricular event (for example

Chile), and more often than not integrated under other disciplines, such as social studies or language courses, and not provided in its own right. In many countries where media education is practised, the production of teaching materials and the training of media educators is very inadequate. As Tufte has observed, "Until recently . . . a great part of media education has been moralizing and playing the part of a guardian who sees the media as a cultural deterioration" (Tufte. 1992:1.)

Moreover, "Media education has often been carried out as literary analysis, which means that the analyses have had the same goal as the traditional analysis of literature, i.e. to teach the children to appreciate the classics, to foster 'good taste' and to teach children to see through 'inferior' products such as, for instance, popular culture". (Tufte. 1992:1). Part of this was motivated by a lack of concern for the culture of ordinary people and a low opinion of the cultural tastes of the working class. Since the early 1990s there is a new trend "which is not based on moral panics. The new trend emphasizes a more relaxed, pluralist and cross-curricular approach to media teaching . . ." (Tufte. 1992: 1).

Media education intends empowerment in the sense of enabling people to participate in processes of public communication, to resist the disempowerment of manipulative media contents, and to express themselves in media language. As Masterman formulates it, "Media education is..an essential step in the long march towards a truly participatory democracy, and the democratisation of our institutions. Widespread media literacy is essential if all citizens are to wield power, make rational decisions, become effective change-agents, and have an effective involvement with the media. . . " (Masterman. 1985: 13).

The Alternative Approach. This approach to empowerment focuses on communication forms, contents, structures, and processes that are distinct from mainstream mass communication although not necessarily totally separate. The approach encompasses a range of activities such as local stations, small community newspapers, minority media, counter-information magazines, theatre groups, pirate radio/TV stations, and alternative contents in mainstream media. In the audiovisual field the alternative approach has recently been termed "tactical television". This genre uses the new features of advanced audiovisual technology (such as portability and affordability) in representations that are challenging and inquisitive, that focus on the powerless and the victims and that provide a bridge between the images of the mainstream media and the people's own images. Community radio and television provides—more than national broadcasting—opportunities for genuine public systems and citizen involvement.

All such efforts attempt to yield countervailing power to the vertical information structures through interactive flows, non-entertainment formats and oppositional contents. This is all important and one should not discourage or underestimate their importance. Yet, there are serious problems that render these efforts insufficient to empower people against the assault of the mainstream media. In many cases the alternative structures end up emulating the dominant model and seem incapable of escaping the technical and aesthetic standards of the professional community. The passion for technology tends to make the alternative approach as vulnerable to the inclination to distort and disinform as the mainstream media. The alternative media tend to remain the playing field of a new class of professionals who like their mainstream colleagues have great difficulty in allowing ordinary people to get too close to either management or production. The scale of operation is very limited compared to the dominant structures and fails to change the operation and content of these structures. Also, the alternative media often not do not reach the captive audiences of the dominant media and may end up preaching to those who were already converted. The alternatives may allow access and participation to people, but usually editorial control remains with the sender. People's participation in decision making remains marginal and often their feedback does not imply any commitment on the part of the addressed. People's involvement depends largely upon "how broadcasters, journalists and publishers will identify with the goals of the people's movement" (Media Development. 1988:1).

The Access and Participation Approach. This approach strives towards people's access to public communication through such means as two-cable TV systems, public access channels, letters to the editor, and through forms of participation in management and production by media users. Particularly in the USA and Canada the availability of cheap printing presses and new cable technologies have stimulated a wide variety of experiences with media access for citizens. The approach also emphasizes the importance of better media employment opportunities for ethnic minorities and women. Particularly during the 1970s a lot of pressure was built up to get the mainstream media to increase the numbers of women in decision making positions. At the end of the United Nations Decade for Women (1976-1985), the World Conference to Review and Appraise the Achievements of the Decade (Nairobi, 1985) reinforced this through the adoption of the Forward Looking Strategies for the Advancement of Women (FLS). The FLS stressed the priority of increasing women's participation in the media. Although detailed data are not yet available, the UNESCO *World Communication Report,* concluded, "that both in terms of overall numbers and of their distribution across and within specific occupations, women's participation is limited. In particular—even taking into account differences of educational level, length of service and range of experience—women are disproportionately excluded from key decision- making posts" (UNESCO. 1989: 209).

The problem with the access and participation approach is that only a very limited margin of empowerment results. The existing structures remain by and large in control and determine the scope of expression. Often the institutional frame is so strong that the newcomer is just co-opted and quickly adapts to the prevailing standards. This does not render the approach a useless strategy. It is important to try to achieve a critical mass of formerly excluded categories into the mass media structures. It is, however, a long and frustrating road to empowerment.

The Technical Assistance Approach. This approach implies that technical assistance is provided in the development of communication facilities. It includes the concrete transfer of funds, technical equipment or training programmes. In earlier chapters attention was given to the problem of communication disparity and the efforts of the world community to redress this through such programmes as UNESCO's IPDC. Among the other specialized agencies that became active in North/South issues was the International Telecommunication Union. (ITU). As early as 1959, the ITU Convention had made reference to the need of cooperation and coordination related to development assistance. The Universal Postal Union (UPU) also got involved with development assistance. It was seen to fall within its mandate to contribute to the organization and development of postal services and the fostering of international postal co-operation. Through UNPD the UPU has contributed to various training programmes and institutions for postal administrations and to the technical co-operation among developing countries. Other UN agencies that became engaged in development assistance in the communications field were the FAO (particularly assistance to development support communication projects), the WHO (projects on media and health/nutrition), UNFPA (communication in family planning), UNICEF (communication for social development projects), and in particular the UNDP. Development cooperation was also initiated in the field of copyright protection. As the payment of copyright fees turned out to be a real problem for poor countries, UNESCO created a system by which governments in rich countries may reimburse their own authors for the publication of their copyrighted materials in poor countries. Additionally the Committee for International Copyright Funds was created by UNESCO to assist the payment of copyright fees through loans. The Joint UNESCO/WIPO Consultative Committee on the Access by Developing Countries to Works Protected by Copyright was established in November 1979 by an agreement between WIPO and UNESCO. One of the tasks of the committee was to improve awareness about the importance of copyright. The main purpose of the work was to facilitate the negotiation and conclusion of publishing and translation contracts between publishers in developing countries and copyright owners who are nationals of industrialized countries.

There are very serious shortcomings in the technical assistance approach. Among them is the fact that the support is almost always too limited. For example, the funding made available by IPDC is almost negligible compared against the scope of resources that would be needed in a serious attempt to diminish communication disparities worldwide.

An even more serious problem is the donor-orientation of most assistance. Funds transfers normally have donor strings attached and equipment is often obsolete or inappropriate. Training tends to impose selected models of professionalism on the recipients. By and large, all efforts in technical assistance to increase the communicative power of people in the South have furthered their disempowerment through economic, technical, and cultural forms of dependency upon donor countries and institutions.

Limits to Empowerment

The different approaches to communicative empowerment are all inspired by such motives as "giving a voice to the voiceless", protecting pupils against the audiovisual assault, or providing people with access to production and management. The importance of this should not be underestimated, since there is enough evidence to show that empowerment strategies can indeed effectively increase people's control over their lives.

In the context of world communication, a basic problem with the approaches to empowerment is the lack of the global dimension. In most cases the approaches do not move beyond the local space. In this way no adequate countervailing power is developed against the global mega communicators.

Also, all the approaches mentioned face the problem that there is a level of inequality implied between the empowering subject and the agent to-be-empowered. Empowerment tends to create new forms of dependency and thus—unintentionally—may cause further disempowerment.

Self-Empowerment

If empowerment—however well-intended—can lead effectively lead to new dependencies, we should question whether we can move from strategies to give voices to the voiceless to strategies by which people speak for themselves. This means that we should understand empowerment as self-empowerment. The term self-empowerment literally means that people make themselves powerful. It refers to a process in which people liberate themselves from all those forces that prevent them from controlling decisions affecting their lives.

In the process of self-empowerment the disempowered participate actively in their own empowerment. They no longer leave decisions to others. They arrive independently at conclusions, they create their own space, define themselves and create chances for unfolding their identities. They demand accountability of those who claim power over them and refuse to see themselves as "beings for others", i.e. as mere buyers or voters. Communicative self-empowerment in the face of the disempowerment by current world communication can take a number of approaches:

People's Media. People's media are owned and controlled by the powerless with the intention to empower themselves. They are a direct confrontation of the disempowered with the dominant communication structure. They select different themes and discourses, tell their own stories and articulate their fears and dreams in the cultural idiom of their own communities. Ordinary people become the active participants in the communication process and actively design their own meaning systems instead of passively consuming the meaning system of the prevailing social order. As Pooranam Demel describes his community work in Tamil Nadu, India, "People's media can be categorised into the indigenous and the non-indigenous. Indigenous people's media would include all traditional folk media, viz, folk theatre, puppetry, mask drama, folk dances, stories, songs, proverbs, jokes, folk games etc. Non-indigenous people's media would comprise liberated use of any non-traditional media with the people in focus. For example, a film or a sound-slide production, or a newspaper report could be used amidst a group of people in order to evoke a discussion on an issue leading to greater conscientisation. Other components of non-indigenous people's media would be street-theatre, photography, videography produced by people; and whole series of non-traditional low cost media such as slogans, writing of handbills, wall-writing, wall-stencil-making, posters/ collages, blackboard journalism, manuscript magazines, low-cost screenprinting, pantograph for enlarging pictures, wall newspapers and cartoons" (Pooranam Demel. 1993: 4).

A concrete example of people's media is the newspaper *Tamania Mars*, established in 1983 by Moroccan women and operated by women in addition to their domestic duties. The newspaper has played a central role in transforming the women's cause to a central public concern. Another illustration is the Bolivian radio station Radio Mallku Kiririya which is controlled by peasants and run for peasants. A special feature of the station is "that it only works at weekends because the peasants who run the station spend the whole week carrying out their normal activities on the land" (Velásquez. 1992: 94). The programmes are participatory and *ad hoc*, "because, as these are not working days, in many cases the villagers have to walk long distances to reach the station" (Velásque. 1992: 94)

People's media such as community radio or TV stations often find it difficult to mobilize local communities after the initial honeymoon period is over. There is real difficulty in getting local communities involved in control, ownership, and management over longer periods of time. People often get bored once the excitement disappears and turn to national or international broadcasting. Community stations also face the strong possibility of powerful parties taking over control. These may be political parties, the military, or the business sector. Financing community stations is a recurrent hassle and often leads to their demise or commercialization. Financial problems forced the Moroccan women's paper *Tamania Mars* out of regular publication. The Moroccan case is illustrative for a more general situation. Rising costs of materials, lack of office space and equipment, and an overall economic deterioration all conspired to stop the operation for one year and to continuously threaten the sustainability of the paper. The financial obstacles add to the general exhaustion members of volunteer's groups are beginning to experience. The women's collective commented in reflection that, "The exhaustion of the members of the group can easily be imagined when to the above are added their responsibilities as mothers and heads of families in a Third World country, where the lack of any facilities to make women's work easier is combined with the weight of social traditions and family responsibilities". (Tamania Mars Collective. 1993: 69).

If no regular funding can be found, the stations will often turn commercial. The subsequent dependence upon advertising revenues creates the almost inevitable pressures on selection of content and choice of target audience. Community stations also need a very strong protection of freedom of speech exactly *vis-a-vis* local powerholders. In many cases the existing legislation provides inadequate protection against local authorities who dislike the people's opinions and ideas.

People's Networks. The currently available computer communication technology makes it fairly easy for PC users around the world to create a public sphere in "cyber space". Using personal computers, modems, and telephone lines new global communities are established. Increasingly, also Third World organizations find it possible to join these forms of horizontal, non-hierarchical exchange that in situations such as the Gulf War have demonstrated to counter censorship and disinformation.

By way of illustration, a letter from a member of a women's organization in Mexico to PeaceNet[1] could be cited. "Until last year we had to ride 24 hours on the bus every 2-3 months to San Antonio, where another Mujer to Mujer member lives, to make marathonic(sic) phone calls to catch up mutually with our key US contacts, plan tours, conferences etc. Long distance phone calls from Mexico have always been prohibitive, and international mail is too slow and undependable". Or a letter from a community-based health project in Nicaragua: "PeaceNet has enabled us to maintain contact with our people there, even when there was not any reliable mail service. It has also provided us a means of exchanging ideas, information and urgent communications with other organizations which share our aims" (in Lewis. 1993: 124).

The current approaches to communicative self-empowerment face several shortcomings. On the economic level, self-empowerment projects often lead an endangered and unstable life. Financial problems may force them out of operation or may drastically amend their character. On the technical level, particularly the new people's networks, are confronted with the fragmented provision of infrastructures in the world. Electricity and telephone lines are not available in many parts of the globe. At the same time, the new technologies are for many people, even the high-tech countries, still too user unfriendly for effective use. The most serious problem in the context of world communication is the local limitation of most people's media. The global dimension often lacks and thus no serious countervailing power against the mega moguls is developed.

The Revolt of Civil Society. The initiative of the reversal of the process of disempowerment must come from people themselves. The media moguls and their political friends will not voluntarily put their power at risk. The transnational service industries, the global telecommunication operators and their large clients, the intellectual property industries or the supporting governments are not likely to insist on the enforcement of rules to counter the disempowering impact of world communication.

A new paradigm for communication that facilitates self-empowerment cannot be state-centric or market-centric. It has to be inspired by civil democracy. Civil society does not only entail rights for its citizens, it also implies duties. The duty to revolt against the worlds of Orwell and Huxley is essential to the democratic process. As citizens can not any longer trust states and markets to accommodate their needs, they will have to take responsibility themselves. They cannot any longer be complacent about the existing communication structures if they want to be relieved from lies and distractions. Only the revolt of civil society can change the disempowerment world communication causes.

The notion of civil society refers to all social transactions in the public and private sphere that are not interfered with by the state. Civil society implies the defence of society against state despotism and it emphasizes the need of a relative autonomy for social life. In most countries civil society is legally rooted in sets of civil rights embodied in constitutions and other forms of legislation. However, it is not sufficient, to stress the bi-polarity of state versus society. Civil society also needs protection against those corporate legal entities that control large parts of national and international economies and global cultural production. The pressures of the market may, just as in the interference by the state, threaten people's capacity for self-governance.

In current political discourse the notion of civil society remains closely tied to the nation-state system. In view of the impotence of individual states to cope with global problems, we need to extend civil society beyond the national borders. It is not enough for a society to establish and defend its local space against domestic forces of the state and the market. As the future of world society is at stake, it should be recognized that we have to develop a global civil society. The struggle for self-empowerment can not be merely local. The local space in which people live is strongly influenced by global developments. The global and the local have to be understood as intimately interlocked.

There are to-day strong trends towards localization in opposition to globalization processes. However, too often these tend to be very parochial, if not dangerously nationalist, ethnic, or fundamentalist. In all these modalities the local loses touch with its broader environment. This may be convenient for those who hold local power and who terrorize their own disempowered fellow-citizens. It puts enormous obstacles on the road to democratic development. Democracy cannot stop at the local border, it has inevitably a broader dimension. Citizenship cannot be limited to a nationality, a state. People have always a double citizenship, in their state and in the world.

As the state in recent times has increasingly proven to be unable to meet peoples' insistent claims for peace, security, equity and unpolluted environments, civil movements have emerged to defend society against the state. These movements have also recognized that conventional forms of political democracy, intertwined with the state system, such as political parties, cannot satisfy these claims. The mobilization of society also targets the non-state powerholders such as market forces that have failed in meeting basic consumer claims for safe, reliable and affordable products.

In the cultural/informational field choices cannot be left to market and state. As the corporations take more and more control of forms of public expression in the performing arts, the museums, the mass media, and the shopping malls, public space needs to be defended against both commercial raiders and the state. By and large, in most societies people are at present not seriously concerned about this. Yet, it would seem to be the task of civil society to be vigilant, with regard to our "secondary environment", in the same way that many people's movements have begun to express concern about the quality of the "primary environment". The time has come for the emerging new social movements to also engage themselves with the issue of the production and distribution of information and culture. If communication is to be an instrument of self-empowerment, it needs to be democratized. This will only become possible when people themselves begin to question whether what world communication delivers to them serves their dignity, liberty and equality.

Today's world communication disempowers people through attractive and effective forms of social control. However, some day the system will run out of luck and its clients will discover that ultimate human fulfilment is not the "triple D satisfaction" of deodorants, diets and detergents. The weakest component of the system are the people who can be manipulated, massaged and indoctrinated, but ultimately not coerced, into switching on their TV sets, their computers or VCRs. It is the continuous anxiety of the "mandarins of world communication" that people decide one day that "enough is enough". This revolt requires an active self-organizing global civil society, that organizes the protection of its interests against the hegemonic, expansionist forces of states and transnational corporations. This means that we interpret civil society not only as a defensive and reactive force, but also as a pro-active movement.

This global civil society should give the concern about the quality of the "secondary environment" priority on its agenda. It is quite obvious that the community of global citizens is geographically dispersed, ideologically fragmented and badly organized. It will be no easy matter to design effective mechanisms to articulate and defend the needs of such a heterogeneous community. However, if we refuse to delegate the decisions about the quality of our "secondary environment" to states and transnational corporations, there is little choice but to begin introducing civil society interests into the arena of world communication. A first step in this global civil initiative could be the worldwide adoption by individuals and movements of a People's Communication Charter. This Charter could provide the common framework for all those who share the belief that people should be active and critical participants in their social reality and capable of governing themselves.

This book concludes with the presentation of a draft of the proposed Charter. This presents an invitation to the readers to respond and to make suggestions for the improvement of the present text. Creating a People's Charter can only be done in a process of dialogue and exchange. The end of this book proposes to be the beginning of such a process.

Summary

World communication affects people's daily lives and the most important trends in world communication converge towards people's disempowerment. They make people powerless *vis-a-vis* the control over their own lives. They create a culture of silence in which people become beings for others. Disempowerment matters since it represents a basic violation of human rights.

The realization of these rights requires that people be capable of taking autonomous decisions. They should be active and critical participants in their social reality and capable of reflection on whether the existing social order should be taken for granted. In disempowerment as well as in the countervailing empowerment strategies communication is a key factor.

The various empowerment approaches have basic flaws. Most important are the implication of new dependencies and the lack of a global dimension. What is needed is people's self-empowerment on a global scale. This means that local communities must reach beyond the borders of their local space and jointly create a global public sphere in which people can freely express themselves, share information, opinions, ideas, and cultural experiences, challenge the accountability of power holders, and take responsibility for the quality of our "secondary environment". For our common future a major global civil initiative in the arena of world communication is critical. The disempowerment of world communication needs a global response. This requires no less than people's self-empowerment towards global citizenship.

Notes

1. PeaceNet was founded in 1985 and is operated by the Institute for Global Communication in San Fransisco. PeaceNet is one of the founding members of the Association for Progressive Communications, established in 1988. APC provides nodes and connected systems across the globe to a large variety of groups and individuals "without respect to race, religion, gender or sexual orientation."

References

Freire. P. (1972). *Pedagogy of the Oppressed*. Harmondsworth: Penguin.

Gerbner, G. (1992). Testimony for the House Judiciary Committee's Subcommittee on Crime and Criminal Justice Oversight Field Hearing on Violence on Television. December 15, 1992, New York.

Hamelink, C.J. (1983 & 1988) (reprint), *Cultural Autonomy in Global Communications*. New York: Longman.

Lewis, P. (1993). *Alternative Media: Linking Global and Local*. Paris: UNESCO. Reports and Papers on Mass Communication. 107.

Masterman, L. (1985). *Teaching the Media*. London: Comedia.

Media Development. Editorial. Issue on "Communication-People's Power." No. 1/1988. London: World Association for Christian Communication.

Pooranam Demel, M.X. (1993). "People's Media: An Alternative." In *Information Bulletin*. Catholic Media Council. 3/93. 2-5.

The Tamania Mars Collective. (1993). In Lewis, P. (1993). *Alternative Media: Linking Global and Local*. Paris: Unesco. Reports and Papers on Mass Communication. 107. 61-72.

Toit, J. du. (1993). "A Media Education Workshop for Women in South Africa". In *Clips*. 4/93. 8-9.

Tomasic, R. (1985). *The Sociology of Law*. London: Sage.

Tomlinson, J. 1991. *Cultural Imperialism*. London: Pinter Publishers.

Tufte, B. (1992). "NewMedia Education Research?" Paper for the Scientific Conference of the International Association for Mass Communication Research. Guarujá, Brazil, August 1992.

Unesco. (1989). *World Communication Report*. Paris: Unesco.

Velásquez, J.R. (1993). "Alternative radio: access, participation and solidarity". In Lewis, P. (1993). *Alternative Media: Linking Global and Local*. Paris: Unesco. Reports and Papers on Mass Communication. 107. 87-96.

People's Communication Charter

Preamble

Signatories of this Charter,

Affirming that communication is basic to the life of individuals and peoples and that communication is crucial in the issues and crises which affect all members of the world community;

Mindful that communication can be used as a force to support the powerful and to victimize the powerless and that communication is fundamental to the shaping of the cultural environment of every society;

Affirming that communication should contribute towards the empowerment of people and that the development of just and democratic societies requires just and democratic communication structures;

Affirming that the formats and contents of communication in most societies tend to disempower people by withholding information, by distorting information, by overwhelming people with overloads of information, or by obstructing people's access to communication channels;

Recognizing that for many people there is no adequate access to channels of communication;

Affirming the need that people develop their own communication channels through which they can speak for themselves;

Recognizing that the rights of communication professionals need to be secured, but that also the information and communication rights of the public need to be protected;

Affirming the right of children to be born in a free, fair, diverse and non-threatening cultural environment;

Recognizing that various forms of censorship, among them interference with media contents by political, military and commercial interests, threaten the independence of information provision;

Recognizing that the consolidation of commercial media into a small number of transnational conglomerates endangers the provision of a pluralism of opinions and a variety of cultural products;

Recognizing that in many countries information and culture are no longer primarily provided as public service but for private profit which may result in an erosion of the public sphere in many societies and the weakening if not disappearance of existing public media;

Acknowledging that the insecurity of journalists working in situations of armed conflict keeps news personnel from having the widest access to sources of information, to travel unhampered, and to transmit information without unreasonable or discriminatory limitation;

Mindful that in spite of the so called 'information revolution', today's reality shows an increasing gap between the world's information-rich and information-poor countries, and between information-rich and information-poor sectors within societies;

Reaffirming with regard to the freedom of information, the social responsibility of the mass media, the development of communication, and the protection of cultural rights the pertinent provisions in international law as listed in the Annexe to the Charter;

Desirous of strengthening current provisions on information, communication, and culture under international law, and in particular the mechanisms for their implementation;

Desirous of promoting greater people's participation in the communication processes of their societies that facilitate political, economic and social development and secure a peaceful and democratic order;

Desirous of creating a cultural environment that protects people's interests and needs;

Convinced that the present Charter contributes to the development of just and democratic communication processes;

Determined to take new steps towards securing a basic human right to communicate for all people;

Agree on the adoption of this Charter and hereby set forth the following guidelines.

Objectives

The Charter intends to contribute to a critical understanding of the significance of communication in the daily lives of individuals and peoples;

The Charter articulates a shared position on communication from the perspective of people's interests and needs;

The Charter aims to bring to (national and international) policy making processes a set of claims that represent people's fundamental right to communicate.

Scope of Application

Signatories to the Charter can be individuals and people's movements (through their representatives) and as such the scope of application of the provisions of the Charter will include all such parties.

Definitions

The term Charter as used in this Charter means a set of guidelines voluntarily adopted by parties and used as their common frame of reference in addressing communication issues.

The term 'parties' as used in this Charter refers to all signatories of the Charter.

The term 'communication' refers to all interactive processes through which individuals and communities share opinions, information, and ideas.

The term 'information' is understood in a very broad sense and includes opinions and ideas presented in entertainment.

The term 'media' refers to publicly or privately owned mass media for print or audiovisual communication.

The term 'information providers' refers to private or public institutions that provide information to the general public and to those individuals who provide information on behalf of such institutions.

The term 'cultural producers' refers to those individuals and institutions who produce and distribute cultural products.

Guidelines

General Standards

Article 1. Fundamental to these standards is the conviction that all people are entitled to the respect of their dignity, integrity, equality, and liberty.

Article 2. People have the right to freedom of expression of opinions, information, and ideas, without interference by public or private parties. For people to exercise the fundamental right to freedom of expression there should be free and independent channels of communication. This means that media should be independent from governmental, political or economic control or from control of materials and infrastructures essential to the production and dissemination of newspapers, magazines, periodicals, and broadcast programs. Free media are pluralistic media. This means that monopolies of any kind are impermissible and that current trends towards the predominantly commercial provision of information and culture should be controlled.

Article 3. People have the right to receive opinions, information and ideas. This implies that people have the right to be informed about matters of public interest. This includes the right to receive information which is independent of commercial and political interests, and the right to receive a range of information and cultural products designed for a wide variety of tastes and interests.

Article 4. People have the right to gather information. This includes the right of access to government information and information on matters of public interest held by public authorities or private interests. There can only be restrictions on access to government and privately held information of public interest if such restrictions are necessary for the protection of a democratic society or the basic rights of others.

Article 5. Since information of public interest will often be gathered on behalf of the people by professionals, effective measures to ensure the safety of journalists on dangerous missions are essential. To be secure in their persons, journalists must be accorded full protection of the law. For journalists working in zones of armed conflict, the appropriate provisions in international humanitarian law should be respected and enforced. In accordance with these provisions journalists must be recognized as civilians enjoying rights and immunities accorded to all civilians in order to conduct their professional duties without harm. Journalists must have safe, unrestricted access to sources of information in order to provide the public with a balanced and adequate reflection of all sides of events. If these rights are not guaranteed, journalists must be able to seek justice through an international body protecting human rights.

Article 6. People have the right to distribute information. This includes fair and equitable access to media distribution channels and to adequate resources and facilities.

Article 7. People have the right of reply. In relation to information concerning individuals published in any medium, the individuals concerned shall have an effective possibility for correction, without undue delay, of incorrect facts relating to them which they have a justified interest in having corrected, such corrections being given, as far as practical, the same prominence as the original expression. Individuals shall have an effective remedy against expressions in any medium which interfere with their privacy except where legitimate public interests justify this interference, or against expressions which constitute violations of their fundamental human rights.

Article 8. People have the right to a diversity of languages. This includes the right to express themselves in their own language. This implies the need to create provisions for minority languages in the media and the need to promote educational facilities to encourage language learning by all people without discrimination.

Article 9. People have the right to protect their cultural identity. This includes the respect for people's free pursuit of their cultural development and the right to express existing cultural variety through the media as well as to receive a variety of cultural expressions. People have the right to the protection of their local cultural space and provisions for the protection of cultural heritage should be established.

Article 10. People have the right to knowledge. This right includes that no one shall be arbitrarily deprived of sources of knowledge. The right shall imply that all peoples and nations have the duty to share with one another their knowledge. The right also entitles everyone to benefit from the protection of the immaterial and material interests resulting from the production of knowledge.

Article 11. People have the right to participate in public decision making on the provision of information. This means that there should be ample scope for public participation in the formulation and implementation of public information policies.

Article 12. People have the right to participate in public decision making on the development and utilisation of knowledge. This means that there should be ample scope for public participation in the formulation and implementation of public policies on the generation and application of knowledge.

Article 12. People have the right to participate in public decision making on the preservation, protection and development of culture. This means that there should be ample scope for public participation in the formulation and implementation of public cultural policies.

Article 14. People have the right to participate in public decision making on the choice, development and application of communication technology. This means that there should be ample scope for public participation in the formulation and implementation of public technology policies and the adoption of technology standards.

Article 15. All forms of public regulation on communication should be transparent. This includes the right of the public to receive full information on public policies in the field of information, knowledge, culture and communication technology. Public transparency should also extend to the practices and organizational structures of large private operators. This means that information on the ownership patterns of large communication corporations should be publicly accessible.

Protective Standards

Article 16. People have the right to the protection by law against interference with their privacy. The media should respect people's right to respect for their private lives. Privacy concerns private, family and home life, physical and moral integrity, honour and reputation, avoidance of being placed in a false light, non-revelation of irrelevant and embarrassing facts, unauthorized publication of private photographs, protection against misuse of rivate communication, protection from disclosure of information given or received by the individual confidentially.

Article 17. People have the right to the protection by law against prejudicial treatment of their person in the media. This right to be treated in non-biased ways implies that reporting by the media should refrain from the use of images that distort the realities and complexities of people's lives or that fuel prejudice by discriminatory descriptions of people and situations, and that neglect the dignity and ability of opponents in national, racial or ethnic conflict. The media should also contribute to the modification of the social and cultural patterns of conduct of men and women, with a view to achieving the elimination of prejudice and all other practices which are based on the idea of the inferiority or the superiority of either of the sexes or on stereotyped roles for men and women.

Article 18. People have the right to respect for the standard of due process in the coverage of criminal cases by the media. This standard implies that the media should not declare defendants guilty before courts have established a verdict of guilt.

Article 19. People have the right to be protected against misleading and distorted information. This right concerns the dissemination of news, the provision of consumer information, and in particular advertising directed at children. News dissemination should be based on accuracy and impartiality. The provision of consumer information should be guided by the consumer's right to protection of health and safety, to protection of economic interests, the right of redress and the right of representation.

Article 20. People's fundamental right to communicate under international human rights law can only be restricted if limitations are prescribed by international law and are necessary in democratic societies.

Accountability and Liability

Article 21. The media should establish mechanisms to address their accountability to the general public. This can be done through self-regulatory bodies set up the media, and through the adoption of editorial statutes in print and audio - visual media in order to strengthen editorial independence. The media should undertake to submit to firm ethical principles guaranteeing the freedom of expression and the fundamental right of citizens to receive accurate and full information on matters of public interest.

Article 22. Media users should organize themselves and establish voluntary associations through which they monitor and assess the performance of the media. These associations could include experts from the academic community.

Article 12. People have the right to hold information providers accountable for the accuracy of their information and establish liability in case inaccurate information causes damage. This should not construe undue limits for the freedom of expression, but if proven in a court of law that an information provider has wilfully disseminated inaccurate or misleading information or has facilitated the dissemination of such information by gross negligence people should have recourse to compensation in case damage can be established.

Education and Development

Article 12. People have the right to acquire the skills necessary to participate fully in public communication. This requires programmes for basic literacy in reading and writing as well as media literacy and critical education about the role of communication in society. This right should enable people to become critical users and producers of information and culture.

Article 25. People have the right to participate in, contribute to and enjoy the development of self-reliant communication infrastructures. This right includes international assistance to the development of independent media, training programmes for professional mediaworkers, the establishment of independent, representative associations, syndicates or trade unions of journalists and associations of editors and publishers, and international co-operation in the field of policy making, regulation and management of media.

People's Responsibilities

Article 26. In accordance with international law all people have the responsibility to strive towards the respect of human rights. In the light of this responsibility we urge all people to contribute to the implementation of the provisions of this Charter. We recommend strongly that users of media should form (national and international) coalitions to promote people's right to communicate.

Enforcement of the Charter

In order to ensure and promote the enforcement of the Charter, Parties shall:

General Provisions

1. Publicize and disseminate the Charter;
2. Ensure the enforcement of the provisions of the Charter within their own movements;
3. Monitor in their own environment the performance of media and information providers and producers of culture in the light of the standards proposed in the Charter;
4. Report regularly about the enforcement of the Charter to a Commission for the Enforcement of the Charter.

Institutional Provisions

A Commission for the Enforcement of the Charter shall be established by all parties adopting the Charter.

Functions of the Commission

1. To coordinate the monitoring of the enforcement of the Charter;
2. To receive complaints about violations of the provisions of the Charter from parties and non-parties to the Charter.
3. To arbitrate in cases of appeal.
4. To specify, extend and adapt the Charter.
5. To coordinate the regular review of the Charter.

Procedures

1. Everyone who observes a violation of provisions of the Charter by parties signatory to the Charter or by media, information providers and producers of culture can lodge a written complaint against those parties with the Commission. The Commission will inform Parties involved through a copy of the letter of complaint and ask them for a defence.

2. The Commission can decide to hear plaintiffs and defendants. Plaintiff and defendant are informed in writing about the judgment the Commission has achieved.

3. The Commission can judge a complaint to be well-founded or unfounded. Arbitration will in cases of appeal will follow an agreed and specified procedure.

4. The review should be re-current and the first formal review should take place not later than five years after adoption of the Charter.

Annexe

With regard to the freedom of information standards are set by Article 19 of the Universal Declaration of Human Rights, by Article 19 of the International Covenant on Civil and Political Rights, by UNESCO Resolutions 3.2. of 1983 and 4.1 of 1991 on the Right to Communicate; by the provisions on information of the 1975 Final Act of the Conference on Security and Co-operation in Europe; by the 1991 UNESCO Declaration of Windhoek; and by Article 13 of the Convention on the Rights of the Child.

With regard to the social responsibility of mass media standards are set by the 1978 UNESCO Declaration on Fundamental Principles concerning the Contribution of the Mass Media to Strengthening Peace and International Understanding, to the Promotion of Human Rights and to Countering Racialism, Apartheid and Incitement to War; by Article 4 of the International Convention on the Elimination of All Forms of Racial Discrimination; by Article 5 of the Convention on the Elimination of All Forms of Discrimination against Women; and by Article 17 of the Convention on the Rights of the Child.

With regard to the development of communication standards are set by the UN Declaration on the Right to Development of 1986; and by UNESCO Resolution 4.1. of 1991 on Communication for development.

With regard to the protection cultural rights standards are set by Article 27 of the Universal Declaration of Human Rights; by Article 15 of the International Covenant on Economic, Social and Cultural Rights; and by the 1966 UNESCO Declaration of the Principles of International Cultural Cooperation.

[This is the fourth draft version of the Charter. The present text has specifically benefited from contributions made by Howard Frederick, George Gerbner, David Goldberg, Wolfgang Kleinwächter, Kaarle Nordenstreng and students at Ohio State University (USA), the American University at Washington DC (USA), the University of Amsterdam (the Netherlands), and the Institute of Social Studies at the Hague (the Netherlands)].

The address for all contributions to further versions of the Charter is:
Centre for Communication & Human Rights
111 Baden Powellweg
1069 LD Amsterdam
Telefax 31.20. 6104821
E mail hamelink@antenna.nl.

Index

Also by Tom Keneally